WELCOME TO HOLLAND

by Emily Perl Kingsley

I am often asked to describe the experience of raising a child with a disability - to try to help people who have not shared that unique experience to understand it, to imagine how it would feel. It's like this......

When you're going to have a baby, it's like planning a fabulous vacation trip - to Italy. You buy a bunch of guidebooks and make your wonderful plans. The Coliseum. The Michelangelo David. The gondolas in Venice. You may learn some handy phrases in Italian. It's all very exciting.

After months of eager anticipation, the day finally arrives. You pack your bags, and off you go. Several hours later, the plane lands. The flight attendant comes in and says, "Welcome to Holland."

"Holland?!?" you say. "What do you mean Holland?? I signed up for Italy! I'm supposed to be in Italy. All my life I've dreamed of going to Italy."

But there's been a change in the flight plan. They've landed in Holland and there you must stay.

The important thing is that they haven't taken you to a horrible, disgusting, filthy place, full of pestilence, famine and disease. It's just a different place.

So you must go out and buy new guide books. And you must learn a whole new language. And you will meet a whole new group of people you would never have met.

It's just a different place. It's slower-paced than Italy, less flashy than Italy. But after you've been there for a while and you catch your breath, you look around.... and you begin to notice that Holland has windmills....and Holland has tulips. Holland even has Rembrandts.

But everyone you know is busy coming and going from Italy... and they're all bragging about what a wonderful time they had there. And for the rest of your life, you will say "Yes, that's where I was supposed to go. That's what I had planned."

And the pain of that will never, ever, ever, ever go away... because the loss of that dream is a very very significant loss.

But... if you spend your life mourning the fact that you didn't get to Italy, you may never be free to enjoy the very special, the very lovely things ... about Holland.

by Emily Perl Kingsley

TABLE OF CONTENTS

These pages may be kept in a binder, printed and dispersed to team members, or printed and posted on classroom bulletin boards for quick reference.

TABLE OF CONTENTS

These pages may be kept in a binder, printed and dispersed to team members, or printed and posted on classroom bulletin boards for quick reference.

INTRODUCTION

Disabilities, Learning
Differences, and
Developmental Disorders

WELCOME AND PURPOSE
LEARNING DIFFERENCES, & DEVELOPMENTAL DISORDERS

DISABILITIES

A physical or mental condition that limits a person's movements, senses, or activities.

LEARNING DIFFERENCES

The unique and individual ways in which some people process new information. In the United States, one in five students has a learning difference, meaning they experience challenges with organization, memory, or attention, especially in academics, such as reading, writing, and math.

DEVELOPMENTAL DISORDERS

A group of conditions due to an impairment in physical, learning, language, or behavior areas. These conditions begin during the developmental period, may impact day-to-day functioning, and usually last throughout a person's lifetime.

IMPORTANCE OF UNDERSTANDING
AND SUPPORTING INDIVIDUALS WITH DIVERSE NEEDS

ENHANCED PROBLEM-SOLVING AND CREATIVITY

Diversity brings different perspectives, experiences, and ideas to the table. By understanding and supporting individuals with diverse needs, organizations can tap into a wider range of talents and viewpoints, which can lead to more innovative solutions and creative approaches to challenges.

IMPROVED LEARNING AND GROWTH

In educational settings, understanding diverse needs allows educators to tailor their teaching methods to accommodate various learning styles and abilities. This personalized approach can facilitate better learning outcomes for all students, regardless of their backgrounds or capabilities.

CULTURAL ENRICHMENT

Embracing diversity exposes individuals to different cultures, traditions, and ways of life. This fosters cultural exchange and appreciation, promoting tolerance and understanding across communities.

IMPORTANCE OF UNDERSTANDING
AND SUPPORTING INDIVIDUALS WITH DIVERSE NEEDS

LEGAL AND ETHICAL OBLIGATIONS:

Many countries have legal frameworks in place to protect the rights of individuals with diverse needs, including laws against discrimination and mandates for accessibility. Understanding and supporting these needs are not just moral imperatives but also legal requirements.

PSYCHOLOGICAL WELL-BEING:

Feeling understood and supported is crucial for an individual's psychological well-being. By acknowledging and accommodating diverse needs, we can help reduce feelings of alienation, isolation, and marginalization, promoting mental health and resilience.

SOCIAL COHESION AND HARMONY:

Building a society that embraces diversity fosters social cohesion and harmony. By understanding and supporting individuals with diverse needs, we can bridge divides, break down stereotypes, and build stronger, more inclusive communities.

ACCOMMODATIONS & MODIFICATIONS

ACCOMMODATION

Accommodations change **how** a student learns the material

COMMON ACCOMMODATIONS

- **Listening** to a book instead of reading it
- Allowed **extra time** to complete a test
- Use of **editing software**

MODIFICATION

Modifications change **what** a student is taught or expected to learn.

COMMON MODIFICATIONS

- **Changing test questions** into simple terms.
- **Adjust the text level** on the novel being read.
- **Pass/no pass** grading

TYPES OF ACCOMMODATIONS

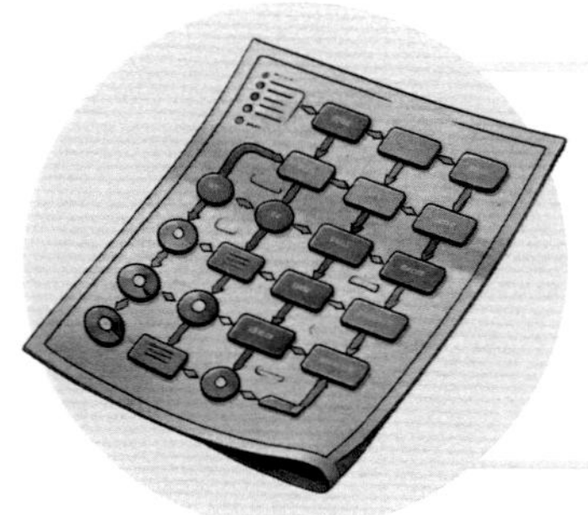

PRESENTATION

Presentation accommodations allow students to access instructional materials in ways that do not require them to read standard print presented in a standard visual format.

SETTING

Setting accommodations change the location in which a test or assignment is given or the conditions of the assessment setting.

RESPONSE

Response accommodations allow students alternatives for completion of activities, assignments, and tests. Students may be permitted to demonstrate their knowledge and skills in alternate ways, or to solve or organize their work using an electronic device or organizer.

TIMING/SCHEDULING

Timing/Scheduling accommodations change the length of time allowed for completion of a test, project, or assignment and may also change the way the time is organized (e.g., breaks):

Listen to audio recordings instead of reading text

Learn content from audiobooks, movies, videos, and digital media instead of reading print versions

Work with fewer items per page or line

Work with text in a larger print size.

PRESENTATION

See an outline of a lesson

Use visual presentations of verbal material...

...such as word webs

Have a "designated reader" — someone who reads test questions aloud to students

Hear instructions spoken aloud

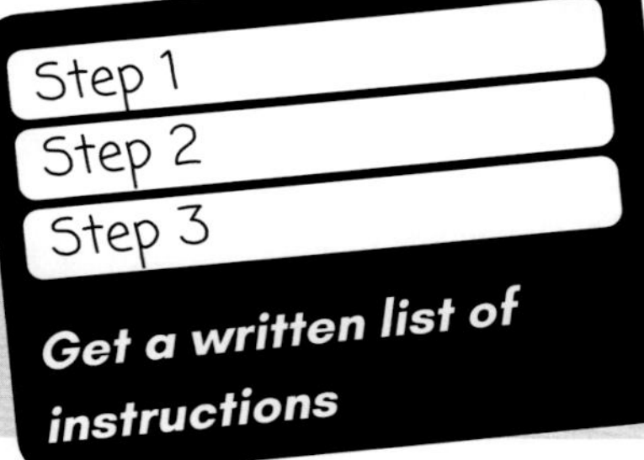

Get a written list of instructions

Record a lesson, instead of taking notes

Get class notes from another student

TIMING/SCHEDULING

- **Take more time** to complete a task, project or test

- Have extra time to process **spoken information and directions**

- Take **frequent breaks**, such as after completing a worksheet

- Take a test in **several timed sessions** or over several days

- Take sections of a test **in a different order**

- Take a test at a **specific time of day**

RESPONSE

Use a **spelling dictionary** or **digital spellchecker**

Capture responses on an audio recorder

A

Give responses in a form (written or spoken) that's easier for them

Use a **word processor** to type notes or give answers in class

Dictate answers to a scribe who writes or types

Use a **calculator** or **table of "math facts"**

SETTING

Take more **time** to complete a task, project or test

Have extra time to process **spoken information and directions**

Take a test at a **specific time of day**

Take sections of a test **in a different order –**

1st	Question 1
3rd	Question 2
2nd	Question 3

Take a test in **several timed sessions** or over several days

Take **frequent breaks**, such as after completing a worksheet

UNDERSTANDING

Different Disabilities
& Disorders

PHYSICAL DISABILITIES

Physical disability indicates any **physical limitations or disabilities that inhibit the physical function of one or more limbs of a certain person**. It can be temporary or permanent. The causes of this kind of disease are various. Any person can acquire it through accident, injury, illness post-surgery effects and heredity.

EXAMPLES OF PHYSICAL DISABILITIES:

CEREBRAL PALSY

A group of disorders that impact a person's ability to move and maintain balance. Cerebral palsy is usually caused by abnormal brain development or brain damage that affects one's ability to control one's muscles. It is the most common motor disability present at birth.

SPINAL CORD INJURIES

Spina cord injury indicates the damages to any part of the spinal cord or nerves at the end of the spinal canal. Result in permanent loss of strength, sensation, and function (mobility and feeling). Causes of spinal cord injury: trauma and diseases

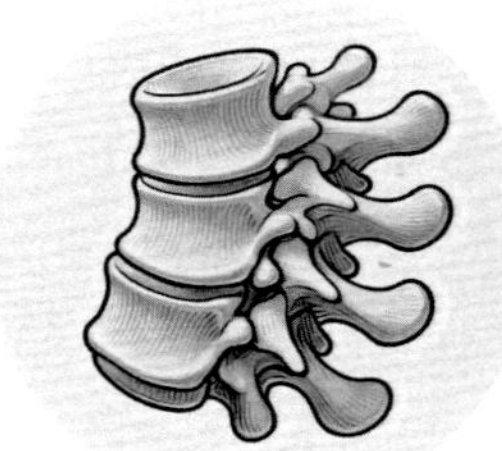

MUSCULOSKELETAL INJURIES

Refer to the damage of muscular or skeletal systems, which is usually due to strenuous activities. They are the most common work-related injuries. Workers often engage in some frequent and repetitive works that require them to hold awkward postures while working and eventually cause the disease to develop.

SPINA BIFIDA

A birth defect that occurs when the spine and spinal cord do not form properly. A type of neural tube defect. The neural tube forms early in pregnancy and closes by the 28th day after conception. Babies with Spina bifida do not have such progress and will suffer from this defect in the spinal and in the bones of the spine.

AMPUTATION

Indicates removal of part of all of a body part that is enclosed by skin. Causes of Amputation: accident, animals attack, warfare, surgery

EDUCATIONAL SUPPORTS
FOR STUDENTS WITH PHYSICAL DISABILITY

ACCESSIBLE CLASSROOM AND SCHOOL FACILITIES

Physical Accessibility

Ensure that all classrooms, restrooms, and school facilities are wheelchair accessible. This includes ramps, elevators, and doors that are wide enough for wheelchair access.

Adjustable Furniture

Provide adjustable desks, chairs, and equipment to accommodate students' various physical needs.

ASSISTIVE TECHNOLOGY

Adaptive Equipment

Utilize tools like specialized keyboards, adaptive mice, voice-to-text software, and other technology that assists with writing, reading, and communication.

Augmentative Communication Devices

For students who have difficulty with verbal communication, provide devices that facilitate communication, such as speech-generating devices or tablets with communication apps.

FLEXIBLE INSTRUCTIONAL STRATEGIES

Differentiated Instruction

Tailor teaching methods and materials to meet the diverse learning needs of students with physical disabilities. This might include using larger print books, audiobooks, or digital resources that are easily accessible.

Hands-On Learning

Incorporate activities that allow students to engage physically, according to their abilities, to enhance understanding and retention of information.

EDUCATIONAL SUPPORTS
FOR STUDENTS WITH PHYSICAL DISABILITY

MODIFIED CURRICULUM AND ASSESSMENT

Curriculum Modifications

Adapt the curriculum to accommodate the physical limitations of students. For example, physical education programs can be modified to include activities in which all students can participate.

Alternative Assessment Methods

Provide alternative ways for students to demonstrate their knowledge, such as oral presentations or projects, if traditional testing methods are unsuitable.

SUPPORT SERVICES

Physical Therapy and Occupational Therapy

Offer services within the school to help students maintain or improve mobility and manage physical challenges related to their disabilities.

Health Aides

Provide trained aides to assist with specific health care needs during the school day, ensuring students can participate in class activities comfortably and safely.

INCLUSIVE EDUCATION

Peer Support and Buddy Systems

Encourage inclusive practices that promote interaction between students with and without disabilities. Peer support programs can help in building social skills and mutual understanding.

Collaborative Learning

Use group work to enable students with physical disabilities to contribute their strengths and learn cooperatively with others.

EDUCATIONAL SUPPORTS
FOR STUDENTS WITH PHYSICAL DISABILITY

PROFESSIONAL DEVELOPMENT FOR STAFF

Training on Disability Awareness

Conduct regular professional development for teachers and school staff to increase their understanding of physical disabilities and effective educational practices.

Specialist Support

Have specialists such as special education teachers or inclusion coordinators available to advise and assist classroom teachers in adapting lessons and materials.

FAMILY AND COMMUNITY INVOLVEMENT

Engagement with Families

Work closely with the families of students with physical disabilities to understand their specific needs and preferences and to keep them informed about their child's progress and school experiences.

Community Resources

Connect families with community resources, such as recreational programs and support groups, that can provide additional support and enrichment.

INDIVIDUALIZED EDUCATION PLANS (IEP)

Tailored Educational Plans

Develop and regularly update an IEP for each student with physical disabilities, outlining specific accommodations, modifications, and support services needed.

DYSPRAXIA

Dyspraxia, also known as Developmental Coordination Disorder (DCD), affects physical coordination and can impact a child's ability to perform daily activities and succeed in school. Understanding the different types of dyspraxia and appropriate accommodations is crucial for supporting children affected by this disorder.

TYPES OF DYSPRAXIA - 3 TYPES

MOTOR DYSPRAXIA

This type primarily affects fine and gross motor coordination. Children with motor dyspraxia may struggle with tasks like writing, tying shoelaces, or participating in sports.

VERBAL DYSPRAXIA

Also referred to as **childhood apraxia of speech (CAS)**, **developmental apraxia of speech** (DAS), or **developmental verbal dyspraxia** (DVD).

A <u>motor speech disorder</u> where a person has difficulty planning and coordinating the movements of the mouth and tongue needed to produce speech sounds.

Not a muscle problem

! It's important to note that CAS is not caused by muscle weakness or paralysis, but rather a problem with the brain's ability to send the correct signals for speech production.

ORAL DYSPRAXIA

This type impacts the voluntary control of movements of the lips, tongue, jaw, and soft palate, affecting oral motor skills like eating, swallowing, and non-speech movements like blowing or sucking.

EDUCATIONAL SUPPORTS
FOR STUDENTS WITH MOTOR DYSPRAXIA

Educational accommodations for motor dyspraxia focus on supporting the student's **coordination and motor skills** challenges, which can impact their ability to perform everyday school tasks such as writing, using scissors, or participating in physical activities. Here are some commonly recommended accommodations:

Assistive Technology

Utilize tools such as word processors for writing assignments to minimize the physical strain of handwriting. Software that features spell-check and predictive text can also be beneficial.

Adaptive Equipment

Provide specialized equipment such as pencil grips, which can make writing tools easier to handle, or keyboards and other adaptive technology for computer use.

Modified Physical Education

Adapt physical education activities or provide alternative options that accommodate the student's motor skills level. This might include tailored exercises that focus on developing coordination in a non-competitive environment.

Extra Time for Tasks

Allow additional time for completing assignments, particularly those that require fine motor skills, to reduce anxiety and provide the student with the opportunity to perform to the best of their abilities.

Instructional Support

Implement teaching strategies that are tailored to the student's learning needs, such as providing step-by-step demonstrations and allowing extra practice time for skill acquisition.

Physical Organization Help

Assist the student in organizing their physical space, ensuring that they have easy access to materials they need frequently. This can help reduce the frustration associated with motor coordination tasks.

EDUCATIONAL SUPPORTS
FOR STUDENTS WITH VERBAL DYSPRAXIA

Educational accommodations for verbal dyspraxia, also known as apraxia of speech, are crucial for supporting students who have **difficulties with the coordination and movement patterns necessary for speech production.** These accommodations aim to enhance the student's ability to communicate effectively within the educational environment. Here are several effective strategies:

Speech-Language Therapy

Collaboration with a speech-language pathologist (SLP) to provide targeted interventions that focus on improving speech production and fluency. Therapy may involve exercises to strengthen the muscles used in speech, as well as techniques to improve articulation.

Augmentative and Alternative Communication (AAC) Devices

Use of technology such as speech-generating devices (SGDs) or apps that facilitate communication. These tools can help students express themselves when verbal communication is challenging.

Extended Time for Responses

Allowing extra time for students to answer questions in class and during tests, as students with verbal dyspraxia may need more time to formulate their responses.

Use of Visual Supports

Incorporating visual aids such as pictures, diagrams, and written prompts to supplement verbal instructions, which can help reduce the student's reliance on speech for understanding.

Training for Staff and Peers

Educating staff and classmates about verbal dyspraxia to foster a supportive learning environment. This includes training on how to use AAC devices and understanding the challenges faced by the student.

Social Skills Groups

Participating in social skills groups led by an SLP or trained educator can help students with verbal dyspraxia develop better interpersonal communication skills.

Modification of Oral Assignments

Adjusting the requirements for oral presentations or allowing alternative formats, such as video presentations or written assignments, can relieve pressure on students with speech difficulties.

EDUCATIONAL SUPPORTS
FOR STUDENTS WITH ORAL DYSPRAXIA

For children with oral motor dyspraxia, educational supports should focus on **visual cues, simplified instructions, flexible deadlines, and opportunities for alternative communication**, while also emphasizing **practice and positive reinforcement** to build confidence and independence.

Allow Alternative Communication Methods

Speech-to-text software: Understood.org recommends using speech-to-text software or dictating to a scribe, which can reduce the burden on motor skills.

Assistive Technology

Consider speech tablets or other devices with speech apps to facilitate communication.

Visual Aids

Utilize picture communication books, visual cues, and "brag books" with pictures and words the student can say or is learning.

American Sign Language (ASL)

If appropriate, explore ASL as a communication option.

Modify Oral Presentations

Reduced Speaking Demands: Allow students to work in small groups for assignments that require speaking, or avoid oral tests altogether.

Extra Time

Provide extra time for oral presentations and allow for breaks during presentations.

No Point Deductions

Avoid deducting points for mispronounced words during oral presentations.

Simplify Instructions

Pair Oral and Written Instructions: Reduce the load on working memory by providing both oral and written instructions.

Use Simple Language

Use clear, concise language and provide visual prompts.

Check for Understanding

Regularly check in with the student to ensure they understand the lesson.

NEURODEVELOPMENTAL DISABILITIES

NEURODEVELOPMENTAL DISORDERS (NDDS) ARE MULTIFACETED CONDITIONS CHARACTERIZED BY IMPAIRMENTS IN COGNITION, COMMUNICATION, BEHAVIOR AND/OR MOTOR SKILLS RESULTING FROM ABNORMAL BRAIN DEVELOPMENT.

EXAMPLES OF NEURODEVELOPMENTAL DISORDERS

Autism Spectrum Disorder (ASD)

Attention-Deficit/Hyperactivity Disorder (ADHD)

Intellectual Disability (ID)

Specific Learning Disorder (SLD)
- dyslexia
- dyscalculia
- dysgraphia

Communication Disorders

Fetal Alcohol Spectrum Disorders (FASD)

Down Syndrome

Tic Disorders

Epilepsy

AUTISM SPECTRUM (ASD)

Monotropism
The tendency to focus on a small number of interests at a given time; having an "attention tunnel," trouble task or topic switching.

Sensory processing
Differences; stimming, becoming over or under-stimulated, may need more or less input from their environment.

May show engagement or attention in subtle ways
(body movement, expression change, repeating what was heard).

Literal interpretation
of language and/or using a blunt/direct communication style.

Attending to one task at a time
possibly benefitting from support and extra time to switch to another task.

Scripting or echolalia
(repeating language that was heard previously)

Differences in play
May prefer a more _self-directed play style_, may play with items in creative or "non-traditional" ways

Talking in depth about a topic of interest
"info-dumping"; struggling to engage with topics outside of their interest(s)

Emotional sensitivity
Emotional regulation challenges, may be hypo or hyper sensitive to others' emotions

Differences in eye-contact
May look away, use peripheral vision, or have a hard time processing information when making eye contact

Relating to others by sharing examples from their own experience
Talking about themself.

- Honesty
- Detail oriented and precise
- Having in-depth and/or expert knowledge in topics of interest
- Strong sense of loyalty & justice
- Passionate
- Logical thinking skills
- Strong memory for facts/figures
- Deep focus when interested
- Innovative
- Perception/appreciation of sensory information
- Recognition of patterns
- Making and using routines
- Living in the present moment
- Strong visual processing skills
- Can be highly social and empathetic

EMPOWERING ABILITIES: A COMPREHENSIVE GUIDE FOR SUPPORTING PEOPLE WITH DISABILITIES

STRATEGIES TO HELP
LEARNERS WITH AUTISM

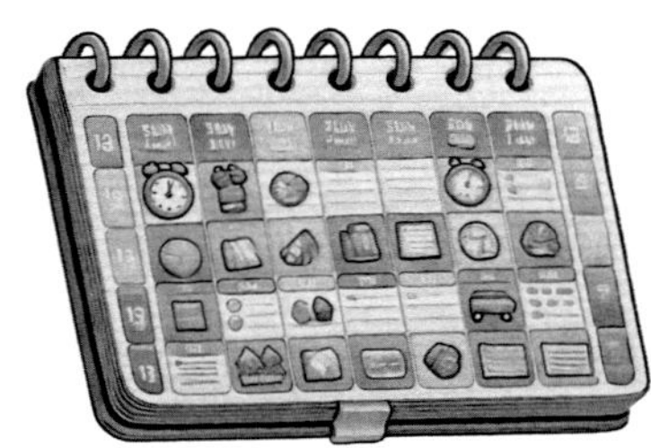

Use visual support, such as pictures, photos, signs, symbols, and gestures, to aid understanding.

Use routine. Let the child know what is happening and when. Use visual timetables, first/then cards, schedules, calendars, etc. This can also help with transitioning from one activity to the next.

Create opportunities for communication and learning. These opportunities can be created throughout the day to embed communication and learning. For example, at snack time, give out a small amount of the snack to create the opportunity to ask for more. Provide choices to create opportunities to communicate, e.g., 'Do you want milk or juice?' This allows the student to hear the words they need and provides an opportunity for the student to communicate (in any way they can).

Use their interests. For example, an interest in trains could be incorporated into various subjects – maths through adding train carriages, English through telling stories about trains, geography through planning trips using train lines, etc.

There may need to be a set time for the student to discuss their interests. During play, use their interests again and follow the child's lead. Let them show you what interests them and how they want to play.

Have fun and be fun. Create engaging opportunities and activities. Creating a shared positive experience with the whole class can create opportunities for friendships and shared experiences. This can be in any way, from a fantastic sensory story to lying on the floor and reading a story. Take photographs throughout to create books of previous activities. The whole class can then use these to look through their shared experiences.

Incorporate Sensory Tools.
Each child will fall on a spectrum of sensory processing and will have sensitivities, avoidance tendencies, and seeking tendencies. There are also likely specific sensory tools that help each child feel regulated.

Some examples of sensory tools:
Weighted lap pad
Fidget
Chewy fidget
Body sock
Noise-canceling headphones
Wobble stool

Keep any instructions short and specific. Ensure you have the child's attention before giving any verbal information. Break down any long instructions into smaller chunks and allow time before repeating the instructions. For example, the instruction 'Get your bag and jacket then wash your hands and sit on the carpet' can be broken down to:

"Get your bag and jacket" ▸ **"Wash your hands"** ▸ **"Sit on the carpet"**

This can also be supported by writing the instructions on a whiteboard (with pictures if available) and ticking them off as the students complete the instructions.

Avoid instructions using any figurative language or anything non-specific. For Example:

This sentence can be misinterpreted:

'Soon we will go outside, and you can hang out with your friends.'

To limit misunderstanding, try:

'In **three minutes**, we will go outside and then you can play with your friends'.

Be flexible and prepared to change your plan. Some things will be trial and error, and what works for one student may not work for another. Try and see how it goes.

Give time. Time may be needed to process an instruction. Count to 10 or 15 before repeating an instruction. Repeating the instruction too soon can mean the student must start processing the information again. Please be sure to use the exact words when repeating the instructions. Time may also be needed to complete tasks in the classroom.

Celebrate the small steps. Each small step that has been achieved may seem small to others, but for you and the student, it represents a considerable achievement.

Support social skills. Social Skills are often an area that children with autism have difficulty with. In particular, the "unwritten" social norms are often the most difficult. Regardless of the skill or subject being taught, social skill practice for children with autism is critical.

Some ways to support social skills:

Social stories	Practice play
Video-modeling	Praise
Visual supports	Role-play.
Social skills training	

INTELLECTUAL DISABILITY (ID)

Difficulty with money management and day to day chores

Signs of this lifelong condition **appear during childhood**

Will need some degree of assistance throughout their lives

Delayed or slowed learning of any kind (such as in school or from real-life experiences)

Distractibility and difficulty focusing

Slower learning of toilet training and self-care activities (bathing, dressing, etc.)

Little or no fear or apprehension of new people (lack of "stranger danger" behaviors)

Trouble using problem-solving and planning abilities

Problems with judgment and critical thinking

Some people may experience minor effects but still live independent lives

Others may have severe effects and need lifelong assistance and support

Difficulties with reasoning and logic

Exhibit challenges in cognitive aspects such as reasoning, learning, and problem-solving

- Resilience
- Creativity
- Compassion and Empathy
- Determination and Motivation
- Compassionate
- Social
- Attention to detail
- Persistence and Adaptability
- Sense of Humor
- Unique Perspectives

EDUCATIONAL SUPPORTS
FOR STUDENTS WITH INTELLECTUAL DISABILITY

INDIVIDUALIZED EDUCATION PROGRAMS (IEP)

Tailored Learning Objectives

Develop an IEP that addresses specific educational needs based on the student's abilities, interests, and family input. Include goals for academic skills and social, communication, and life skills.

Regular Reviews

Periodically assess and adjust the IEP to reflect the student's progress and changing needs.

FUNCTIONAL CURRICULUM

Practical Skills Focus

Incorporate a curriculum that teaches practical life skills, such as personal care, job responsibilities, and money management, which are essential for independence.

Context-Based Learning

Teach academic concepts through their application in real-life situations to enhance understanding and relevance.

INCLUSIVE EDUCATION

Mainstreaming

Whenever possible, include students with intellectual disabilities in general education classrooms with appropriate support to promote social interactions and exposure to age-appropriate activities.

Peer Supports

Utilize peer tutoring and inclusive group activities to foster relationships and enhance learning through social interaction.

EDUCATIONAL SUPPORTS
FOR STUDENTS WITH INTELLECTUAL DISABILITY

SOCIAL SKILLS TRAINING

Explicit Instruction

Teach social skills explicitly, using role-playing, social stories, and other interactive methods to demonstrate appropriate social behavior.

Supervised Socialization

Organize supervised activities that allow students to practice social skills in a safe and supportive setting.

COLLABORATIVE TEAM APPROACH

Multi-Disciplinary Team

Involve a team of professionals, including special educators, speech therapists, occupational therapists, and psychologists, to provide a comprehensive support system.

Family Involvement

Actively engage families in the educational process, encouraging their input and sharing strategies that can be reinforced at home.

TRANSITION PLANNING

Early and Ongoing Planning

Start planning for transitions, such as from school to adult life, early to ensure a smooth changeover. Focus on vocational training and employment opportunities as part of this planning.

Community Integration

Teach skills that help students participate in their communities, such as using public transportation, interacting in social settings, and accessing community resources.

EDUCATIONAL SUPPORTS
FOR STUDENTS WITH INTELLECTUAL DISABILITY

DIFFERENTIATED INSTRUCTION

Adapt Teaching Methods

Use varied instructional strategies tailored to the student's learning style and cognitive level, such as visual aids, hands-on activities, and technology-assisted learning.

Pace and Level Adjustments

Modify the pace of instruction and complexity of materials to suit the student's processing speed and comprehension level.

USE OF ASSISTIVE TECHNOLOGY

Communication Aids

Employ devices and software that aid communication for non-verbal students or those with limited communication skills.

Educational Technology

Use tablets, interactive software, and specialized apps to enhance learning and engagement.

BEHAVIORAL SUPPORTS

Positive Reinforcement

Implement a positive reinforcement system to encourage desirable behaviors and learning engagement.

Consistent Structure

Provide a structured learning environment that helps students understand expectations and routines.

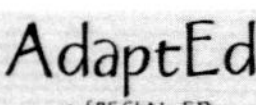

ATTENTION-DEFICIT / HYPERACTIVITY
DISORDER (ADHD)

Talkative
May blurt out or interrupt

High energy
May have a very active body and/or mind.

May get distracted easily, or pay attention to details unrelated to the task at hand.

Challenges with self-starting
May procrastinate.

Sensory processing differences
Fidgeting or stimming (may become overstimulated or under stimulated).

Tendency to miss details, but may recognize the main idea or whole picture.

Time agnosia
Challenges with time judgement.

Organization may be a challenge
Commonly are visual organizers.

Emotional sensitivity & emotional regulation challenges
May have Rejection Sensitive Dysphoria, which is intense sensitivity and emotional pain related to real or perceived rejection or criticism

COMMON STRENGTHS

- Intense focus when interested (hyperfocus)
- Creativity
- Spontaneity
- Energy
- Compassionate
- Passionate
- Multi-tasking
- Willingness to take risks
- Innovative

- Strong sense of humor
- Working under pressure
- Project oriented
- Talkative
- Good problem solving skills
- Curious
- Persistent
- Diverse in hobbies and skillsets
- Strong sense of justice

TYPES OF ADHD

ADHD, INATTENTIVE TYPE

Primarily characterized by **unique attention patterns**, such as finding it challenging to **focus on tasks** that lack interest, **following detailed instructions**, and **organizing tasks**. People with this condition often thrive in **stimulating environments** and demonstrate **high creativity**, even if they sometimes find **traditional organization methods** less effective.

ADHD, HYPERACTIVE / IMPULSIVE TYPE

Primarily characterized by **abundant energy** and **spontaneity** (e.g., **difficulty sitting still, talkative, fidgeting, high energy**) and a tendency to **act quickly** without always considering the consequences (e.g., frequently **interrupting others, jumping into situations, blurting out answers**).

ADHD, COMBINED TYPE

ADHD, Combined Type, is a form of attention-deficit/hyperactivity disorder where **individuals exhibit both inattentive and hyperactive-impulsive traits.** People with this type often have u**nique attention patterns** and **abundant energy**, allowing them to excel in **dynamic and stimulating environments**. They may face challenges with **traditional organization** and **focus** but frequently demonstrate **high creativity, quick thinking, and adaptability.**

EDUCATIONAL STRATEGIES

ATTENTION DEFICITS

PRESENTING PROBLEM : DIFFICULTY SUSTAINING ATTENTION

INTERVENTIONS :

1 REDUCE DISTRACTIONS.
Try to minimize distractions and disruptions in the classroom.

For example, you can seat the person away from doors and high-traffic areas and put distracting displays behind them.

You can also try to be **physically close** to students when you speak and make eye contact.

2 SCHEDULE MOVEMENT BREAKS.
Brain breaks can help refresh thinking patterns and break up a dull routine.

3 SET A CLEAR ROUTINE.

4 GIVE CLEAR DIRECTIONS.

5 Help the person **organize** their **materials.**

6 Encourage students to **get involved** with their work.

For example, they could underline reading material or draw cartoons to illustrate vocabulary words.

STRATEGIES TO HELP
LEARNERS WITH ADHD

Give **clear**, written, and verbal **directions**

Chunk long-term projects.

Use a timer for work sessions.

Spend time building **confidence**.

- [ ] Give extra opportunities for **movement.**
- [ ] Consider **flexible seating** options.
- [ ] **Provide fidgets** and teach how to use them.
- [ ] Set up a **work station** in each class.

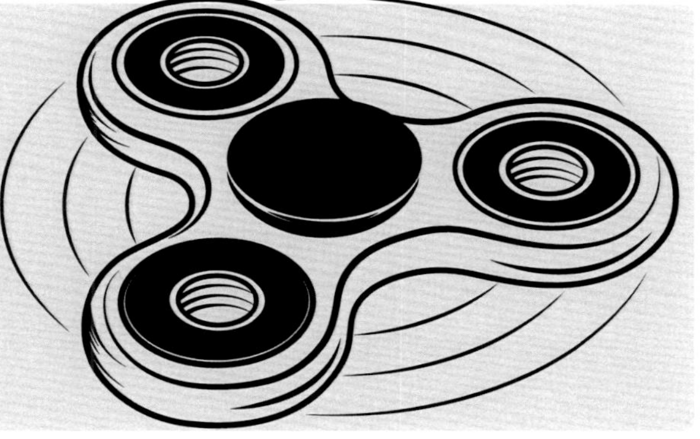

Schedule an organization **check-in time.**

Use a **thought journal** to share ideas.

Teach **executive functioning** skills.

Teach and practice **predictable routines.**

AdaptEd
4 SPECIAL ED

OVERVIEW OF SLD TYPES

DYSLEXIA

Dyslexia is a **learning difference** that affects a person's **ability to read, write, and spell**. It's a **neurological variation** often passed down through families, making it **genetic**. People with dyslexia have brains that **process language uniquely**, leading to **distinctive approaches** to reading and writing despite **normal intelligence**.

DYSGRAPHIA

Dysgraphia is a **learning difference** that affects **writing abilities**. It involves **unique challenges** with **handwriting, spelling, and organizing thoughts on paper**. People with dysgraphia may have difficulty **forming letters, spacing words, and writing legibly**, yet they possess **normal intelligence** and often exhibit **creativity** and **problem-solving skills**.

DYSCALCULIA

Dyscalculia is a **learning difference** that affects a person's **ability to understand and work with numbers**. It involves **unique challenges** with **basic arithmetic, number sense, and math-related concepts**. People with dyscalculia may find tasks such as **calculating, measuring, and remembering math facts** challenging, yet they possess **normal intelligence** and often excel in **creative** and **non-linear thinking**.

A CLOSER LOOK AT DYSLEXIA

RESEARCH INSIGHTS ON DYSLEXIA

Dyslexia, though uncommon, is widespread enough to be well-known, affecting about **7% of people worldwide** equally across **all sexes and races**. The exact cause of dyslexia isn't clear, but several factors provide clues about its occurrence.

GENETICS

Dyslexia is highly genetic and runs in families. A child with a dyslexic parent has a **30% to 50% chance of inheriting it**. Genetic conditions like Down syndrome can also increase the likelihood of dyslexia.

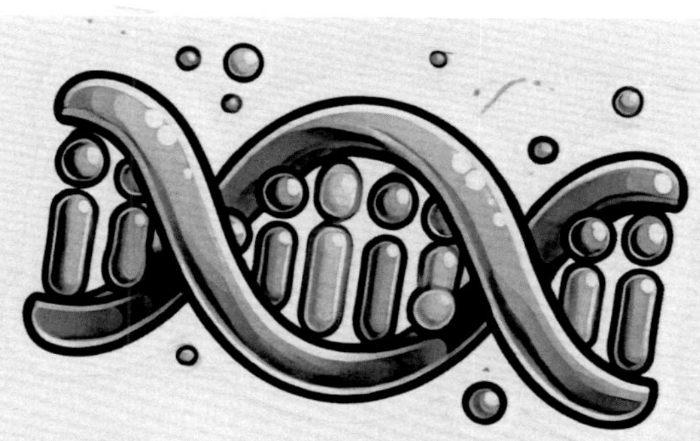

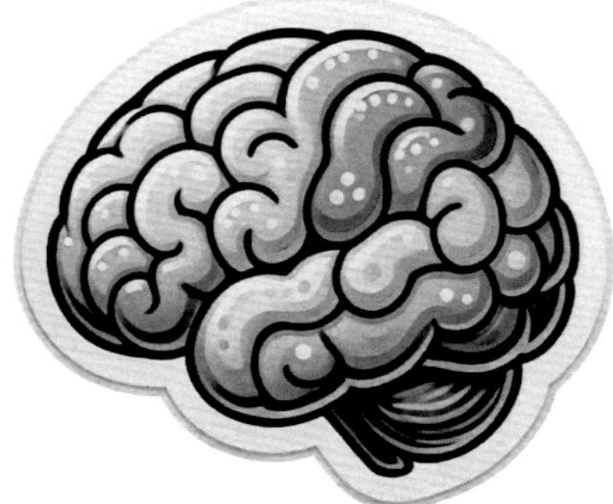

DIFFERENCES IN BRAIN DEVELOPMENT AND FUNCTION

People with dyslexia are neurodivergent, meaning their brains form and function uniquely. Research shows different **brain structures, functions, and chemistry** in individuals with dyslexia.

DISRUPTIONS IN BRAIN DEVELOPMENT

Infections, toxic exposures, and other events can **disrupt fetal development**, increasing the likelihood of dyslexia later in life.

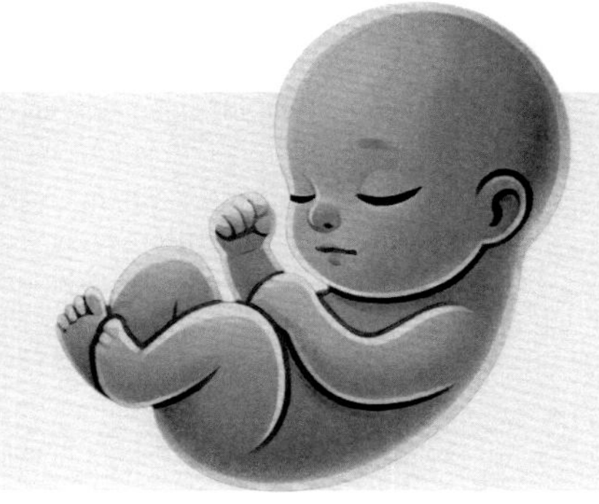

DYSLEXIA INTERVENTION

Recent research on dyslexia suggests that the most successful interventions are rooted in an approach developed in the 1920s called **Orton-Gillingham**. Named after its creators, a neuropsychiatrist and an educator, this method emphasizes **systematic reading intervention**.

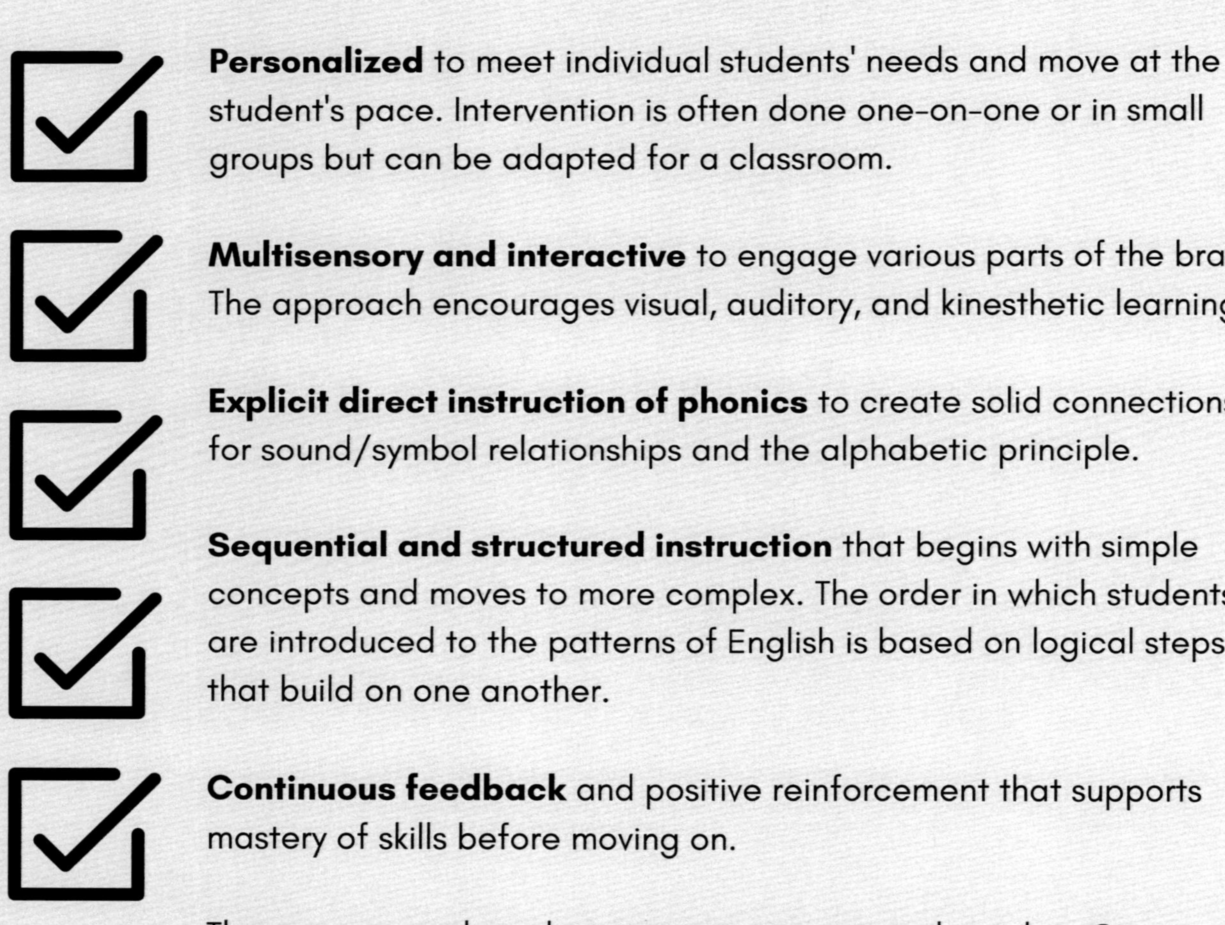

THIS CONSISTS OF THE FOLLOWING COMPONENTS:

- **Personalized** to meet individual students' needs and move at the student's pace. Intervention is often done one-on-one or in small groups but can be adapted for a classroom.

- **Multisensory and interactive** to engage various parts of the brain. The approach encourages visual, auditory, and kinesthetic learning.

- **Explicit direct instruction of phonics** to create solid connections for sound/symbol relationships and the alphabetic principle.

- **Sequential and structured instruction** that begins with simple concepts and moves to more complex. The order in which students are introduced to the patterns of English is based on logical steps that build on one another.

- **Continuous feedback** and positive reinforcement that supports mastery of skills before moving on.

There are several reading instruction programs based on Orton-Gilligham. The key to these programs is that they are provided to the child/adult based on the publisher-recommended time per week and implemented with consistency and fidelity.

AdaptEd
4 SPECIAL ED

ACCOMODATIONS FOR
DYSLEXIA

INTRODUCING NEW CONCEPTS

Pre-teach new concepts and vocabulary.

Provide the student with **typed notes** or an **outline** of the lesson to help with taking notes.

Provide **advance organizers** to help the student follow along during a lesson.

Provide a **glossary** of content-related terms.

Use **visual** or **audio support** to help the student understand written materials in the lecture.

GIVING INSTRUCTIONS

Help the student **break assignments into smaller steps.**

Arrange worksheet problems from **easiest to hardest.**

Give **self-monitoring checklists** and guiding questions for reading comprehension.

Highlight key words and ideas on worksheets for the student to read first.

Show examples of correct and completed work to serve as a model.

Give step-by-step directions and **read written instructions out loud.**

Simplify directions using key words for the most important ideas.

Provide a **rubric** that describes the elements of a successful assignment.

Check in frequently to make sure the student understands and can repeat the directions.

ACCOMODATIONS FOR
DYSLEXIA
COMPLETING TESTS AND ASSIGNMENTS

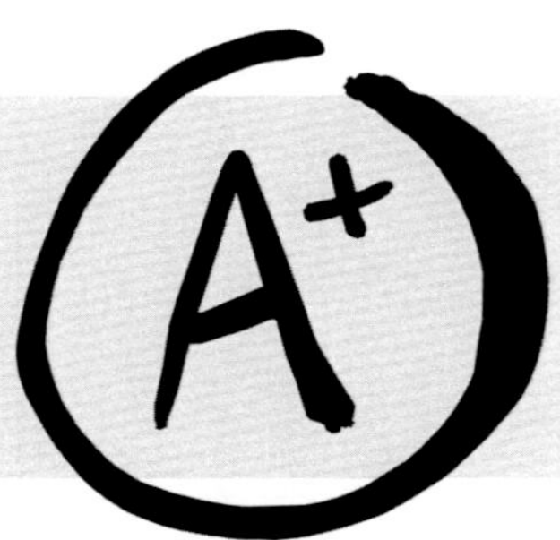

Grade the student on the content that needs to be mastered, not on things like spelling or reading fluency.

Allow understanding to be demonstrated in different ways, like oral reports, posters, and video presentations.

Provide sentence starters that show how to begin a written response.

Provide a quiet room for taking tests, if needed.

Provide extended time for taking tests.

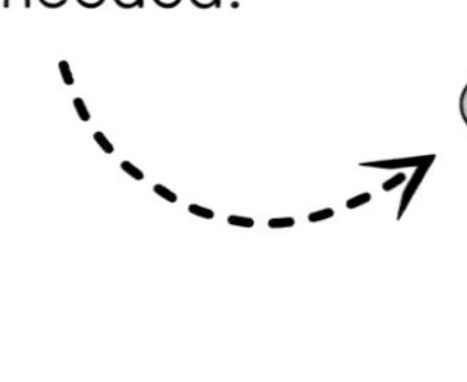

Provide different ways to respond to test questions, like saying the answers or circling an answer instead of filling in the blank.

A CLOSER LOOK AT
DYSGRAPHIA

Dysgraphia is a **neurological condition** and **learning difference** where individuals face **unique writing challenges**. This can include the **physical act of writing** or **translating thoughts into words**. With targeted interventions, new writing strategies can be developed.

WRITING IS A COMPLEX PROCESS INVOLVING MANY SKILLS AND BRAIN FUNCTIONS, INCLUDING:

- Fine motor skills
- Spatial perception (ability to perceive the space around you)
- Working memory (ability to hold and manipulate information in your mind)
- Orthographic coding (ability to form, store, and recall letters, numbers, and symbols)
- Language processing
- Conceptualization
- Organization

Due to this complexity, dysgraphia is a broad term for various writing challenges and can be difficult to diagnose.

Dysgraphia generally appears when children first learn to write, known as **developmental dysgraphia**. It can also develop suddenly after head or brain trauma, referred to as **acquired dysgraphia.**

Dysgraphia is classified as a **"specific learning disorder,"** specifically a **"specific learning disorder in written expression."**

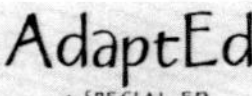
AdaptEd
4 SPECIAL ED

ACCOMODATIONS FOR
DYSGRAPHIA

CLASSROOM MATERIALS AND ROUTINES

Allocate **additional time** for the student to take notes and transcribe materials.

Offer a variety of pencil grips or alternate types of pens and pencils to determine which is most comfortable and effective for the student.

Distribute handouts to minimize the need for copying from the board.

Furnish typed copies of **classroom notes or lesson outlines** to facilitate note-taking for the student.

Provide **graph paper or lined paper** positioned sideways to aid in aligning math problems accurately.

Supply paper featuring different-colored or raised lines to assist with letter formation and spacing.

Permit the use of an audio recorder or laptop during class sessions

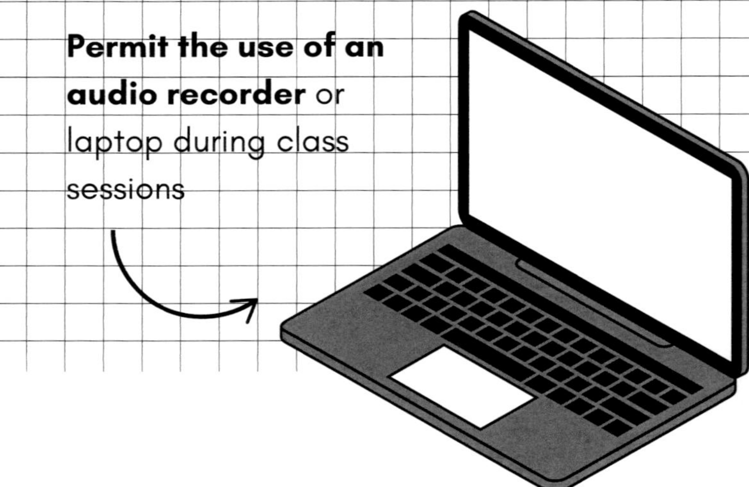

ACCOMODATIONS FOR
DYSGRAPHIA

GIVING INSTRUCTIONS

Issue paper assignments with essential details such as name, date, and title pre-filled.

Supply necessary information in advance to facilitate early start on writing assignments.

Assist the student in breaking down writing tasks into manageable steps.

Furnish a rubric detailing grading criteria for each step of the assignment and offer explanations.

Provide examples of completed assignments to serve as references.

Offer alternative response methods, such as oral reports

COMPLETING TESTS AND ASSIGNMENTS

Modify test formats to minimize handwriting by utilizing options like "circle the answer" or "fill in the blank" questions.

Assess students based on their understanding of the material rather than focusing on handwriting or spelling.

Offer the option of using a scribe or speech-to-text technology for test answers and writing assignments.

Allow students to choose between printing or using cursive for handwritten responses.

Permit students to have a "proofreader" check for errors.

Provide extended time for completing tests.

Offer a quiet testing environment for students who require it.

DYSCALCULIA

MATH DYSCALCULIA

Dyscalculia is a learning disorder that affects a person's ability to understand number-based information and math. People who have dyscalculia struggle with numbers and math because their brains don't process math-related concepts like the brains of people without this disorder. However, their struggles doesn't mean they're less intelligent or less capable than people who don't have dyscalculia.

WHAT ARE THE SYMPTOMS OF DYSCALCULIA? (PRE-K/ K)

Has trouble learning to count and skips over numbers long after kids the same age can remember numbers in the right order

Struggles to connect a number to an object, like knowing that "3" applies to groups of things like three cookies, three cars, or three kids

Struggles to recognize patterns, like smallest to largest or tallest to shortest

Has trouble understanding number symbols, like making the connection between "7" and the word seven

Doesn't seem to understand the meaning of counting for example, when you ask for five blocks, your child just hands you a large group of blocks, rather than counting them out

SCHOOL-AGE CHILDREN (PRIMARY/GRADE/ELEMENTARY SCHOOL)

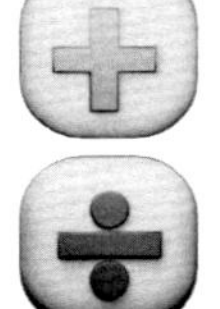
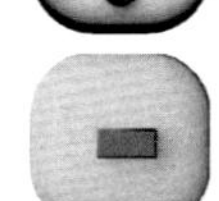

- **Has trouble learning and recalling basic math facts**, like 2 + 4 = 6
- **Still uses fingers to count** instead of using more advanced strategies (like mental math)
- **Struggles to identify math signs** like + and − and to use them the right way
- **Has a tough time understanding math phrases**, like greater than and less than
- **Has trouble with place value**, often putting numbers in the wrong column

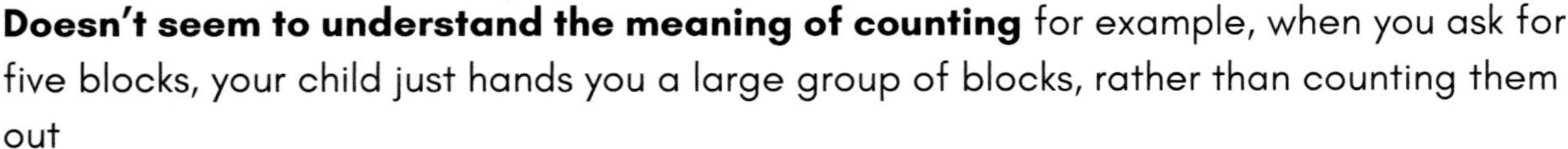

AdaptEd
4 SPECIAL ED

DYSCALCULIA (CONT.)

TEENAGERS (SECONDARY SCHOOL- OR HIGH SCHOOL-AGE) AND ADULTS

- **Struggles to read charts and graphs**
- **Has trouble applying math concepts to money**, like making exact change and figuring out a tip
- **Has trouble measuring things** like ingredients in a recipe or liquids in a bottle
- **Lacks confidence in activities** that require understanding speed, distance, and directions, and may get lost easily
- **Has trouble finding different approaches to the same math problem**, like adding the length and width of a rectangle and doubling the answer to solve for the perimeter (rather than adding all the sides)

EMOTIONAL SYMPTOMS

People with dyscalculia may show emotional symptoms when faced with situations where math is necessary. Those emotional symptoms often include:

- **Anxiety** (including test anxiety) or even panic.
- **Agitation, anger or aggression** (such as temper tantrums in younger children).
- **Fear** (including a fear or even phobia of going to school).
- **Physical symptoms** of any of the above (nausea and vomiting, sweating, stomachache, etc.)

AdaptEd
4 SPECIAL ED

DYSCALCULIA

GIVING INSTRUCTIONS AND ASSIGNMENTS

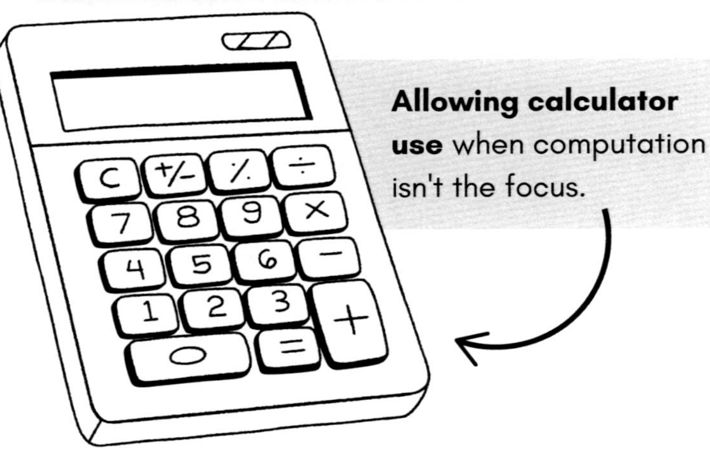

Allowing calculator use when computation isn't the focus.

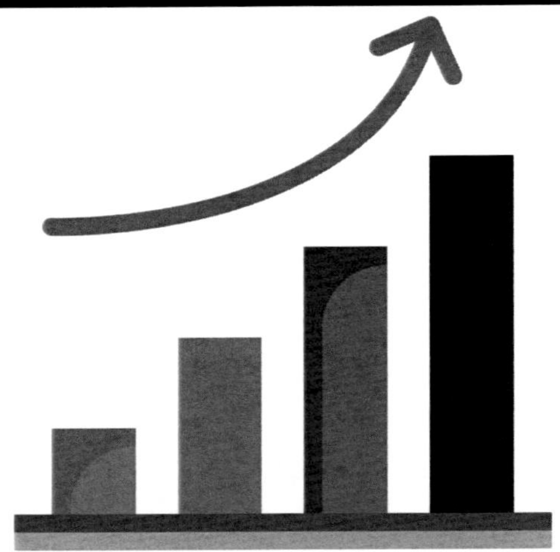

Emphasizing keywords and numbers in word problems.

Breaking down large assignments into smaller tasks.

Extending time for lengthy assignments or projects.

Utilizing separate worksheets for word and number problems.

Using extra paper to focus on one problem at a time.

Offering ample space for writing problems and solutions.

Offering charts of math facts or multiplication tables for reference.

Incorporating visual aids or manipulatives during problem-solving activities.

Supplying rubrics outlining assignment elements.

Including tables, graphs, or number lines to reduce information overload.

Providing clear step-by-step instructions for problem-solving.

Breaking worksheets into manageable sections.

Providing checklists for multi-step procedures.

Implementing checkpoints in large assignments for feedback.

AdaptEd
4 SPECIAL ED

ACCOMODATIONS FOR
DYSCALCULIA

INTRODUCING NEW CONCEPTS/LESSONS

Review previously learned material before introducing new concepts.

Encourage students to articulate their problem-solving process through self-talk.

Allow students to utilize written charts or sketches to solve problems.

Provide graph paper to assist in aligning numbers and problems accurately.

Furnish a list of math formulas taught in class for reference.

Utilize manipulatives such as coins, blocks, and puzzles to illustrate mathematical concepts, with virtual manipulatives for higher grade levels.

Employ attention-grabbing phrases to emphasize the importance of new concepts.

Use real-life examples to demonstrate the relevance of mathematical concepts.

Check in regularly with students to ensure comprehension.

Utilize graphic organizers to facilitate organization and breakdown of math problems into manageable steps.

Demonstrate tasks visually and provide tangible examples for students to refer back to during practice.

COMPLETING TESTS AND ASSIGNMENTS

Give extended time on assessments.

Provide a quiet room with limited distractions for taking tests.

Give access to a calculator when computation is not being assessed.

Limit the number of problems on one page and give plenty of space to solve each problem.

COMMUNICATION DISORDERS

A child with a communication disorder has trouble communicating with others.
He or she may not understand or make the sounds of speech.
The child may also struggle with word choice, word order, or sentence structure.

COMMON DIFFERENCES

SYMPTOMS

- Not speaking at all
- Limited word choice for his or her age
- Trouble grasping simple directions or naming objects

Young children with these disorders can speak by the time they enter school. But they still have problems with communicating.

School-aged children often have problems understanding and making words.

Teens may have more trouble understanding or expressing abstract ideas.

TREATMENT

A speech-language pathologist will work with your child to improve his or her communication skills.

Treatment is often a team effort.

Parents, teachers, and mental health experts may also be involved.

Treatment may include:
- Individual or group support
- Special classes

COMMUNICATION STRATEGIES

THERE ARE MANY WAYS TO
COMMUNICATE

THERE ARE SO MANY WAYS TO COMMUNICATE AND THEY ARE <u>ALL</u> VALID!

- **Speech**
- **Echolalia** (repeating words/phrases/scripts that have been heard previously)

Gestures or physically taking a person's hand and leading them.

Displays of **emotion**

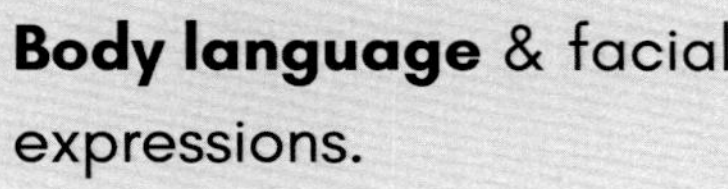

Body language & facial expressions.

Use of **icons/symbols**/AAC

WE ALL USE MULTIPLE METHODS OF COMMUNICATION EVERYDAY.

Some individuals may be nonspeaking, have differences in their verbal speech, or be unable to consistently rely on their communication in different circumstances.

AS EDUCATORS AND ALLIES, WE CAN SUPPORT COMMUNICATION BY:

- Promoting **multimodal** communication
- Recognizing that ALL communication is essential. By accepting how the person communicates, you are teaching them that communication is valuable and powerful
- Providing unrestricted access to AAC

- Modeling language and AAC usage
- Respond to all communication attempts
- **Allow time** for the person to **process** the information.
- Do not use **baby talk** or talk down to a person

COMMUNICATION STRATEGIES (CONT'D)

GESTURES AND NONVERBAL COMMUNICATION

Including gestures such as pointing, nodding, and focused eye contact can help children with disabilities understand messages. Parents, family members, and friends may need to exaggerate or prolong their gestures, especially in the beginning, to promote comprehension. Children generally like responding to exaggerated nonverbals with their movements and gestures, but for children with disabilities, gestures are almost necessary.

READ TO THEM AND TALK TO THEM OFTEN.

Practice makes perfect, according to the old saying, and this is undoubtedly a good one for children with disabilities who are learning better communication strategies. The first step to learning a language is listening, and we cannot expect a child to communicate well if we do not teach them to understand. Exposure to communication is a crucial element of learning.

CONSTANTLY EXPLAIN.

In the grocery store, talk to the child at every step. Count the apples as you put them in plastic bags, read the items off the list and check them off with the child, and finally, allow the child to help you organize and store groceries when you get home. This will enable you to repeat the items to the child repeatedly, promoting learning and teaching him or her about grocery shopping along the way. It can be applied to other aspects of your routine as well.

COMMUNICATION STRATEGIES (CONT'D)

CHANGE IT UP A BIT.

While you certainly want to begin with simple language, you will eventually want to expand your child's vocabulary if he or she can. Challenge your vocabulary by mixing your words a bit. Start small. Use "the other words" from time to time. Rather than saying to your child to go through the door, tell him or her to enter through it. Expansion of vocabulary challenges the thought process and helps a child feel confident in communication skills.

USE PICTURES.

Like flashcards, pictures can challenge the memory. Associating still pictures with words can help the child associate words with the real world. You can use pictures with single items rather than those with busy backgrounds. As the child learns, you may introduce more challenging scenery or pictures in which children may identify several objects.

REALIZE AND RESPECT THEIR DIFFERENCES AND LIMITATIONS.

Challenging children can give them opportunities to succeed, but parents can also overdo it. The child will let you know when he or she is ready to move on to another adventure in language.

FETAL ALCOHOL SPECTRUM DISORDER

A group of conditions that can occur in a person who was exposed to alcohol before birth.
Can include physical problems and problems with behavior and learning

COMMON DIFFERENCES

Low body weight

Poor coordination

Hyperactive behavior

Poor memory

Difficulty in school (especially with math)

Learning disabilities

Speech and language delays

Intellectual disability or low IQ

Poor reasoning and judgment skills

Sleep and sucking problems as a baby

Vision or hearing problems

Problems with the heart, kidneys, or bones

Shorter-than-average height

Abnormal facial features, such as a smooth ridge between the nose and upper lip (this ridge is called the philtrum)

Citation: https://www.cdc.gov/ncbddd/fasd/index.html

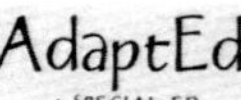

EDUCATIONAL SUPPORTS
FOR STUDENTS WITH FASD

STRUCTURED LEARNING ENVIRONMENT

Consistency and Routine

Provide a predictable daily schedule and clear classroom routines to help students feel secure and understand what is expected of them.

Organized Space

Keep the classroom environment organized and clutter-free to minimize distractions and help maintain focus.

INDIVIDUALIZED EDUCATION PLANS (IEP)

Customized Goals

Develop an IEP that addresses both academic and behavioral needs based on the child's specific strengths and challenges.

Regular Assessments

Continuously assess and adjust educational strategies to meet evolving needs and to accommodate various developmental stages.

EXPLICIT INSTRUCTION

Clear and Concise Instructions

Use simple, direct language with visual supports if necessary. Repeat instructions and check for understanding by asking the student to repeat the information.

Step-by-Step Learning

Break down tasks into smaller, manageable steps and provide frequent feedback to help students process and retain information.

EDUCATIONAL SUPPORTS
FOR STUDENTS WITH FASD

VISUAL AIDS AND SUPPORTS

Use of Visuals

Incorporate charts, graphs, and pictures to support text and verbal instructions. Visual schedules can help students understand and manage transitions between activities.

Technology Integration

Employ educational software and apps designed to enhance learning through visual and interactive methods.

BEHAVIORAL SUPPORT

Positive Reinforcement

Implement a system of positive reinforcement for appropriate behaviors and academic achievements. Focus on specific praises that acknowledge the effort and improvement.

Behavior Management Plans

Create specific, proactive strategies for managing challenging behaviors in a consistent and supportive manner.

SOCIAL SKILLS TRAINING

Structured Social Interactions

Use role-playing games and social stories to teach appropriate social behaviors and interaction skills.

Peer Group Activities

Facilitate small group interactions with peers who can model appropriate social behavior.

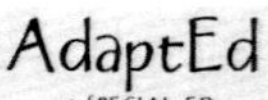

EDUCATIONAL SUPPORTS
FOR STUDENTS WITH FASD

MULTI-SENSORY APPROACHES

Incorporate Multiple Senses
Use teaching methods that involve touch, movement, and visual elements to enhance understanding and retention.

Hands-On Activities
Engage students with hands-on learning experiences that allow them to manipulate materials and participate actively in their learning process.

COLLABORATION WITH SPECIALISTS

Regular Consultations
Work closely with occupational therapists, speech therapists, and special education experts who can provide additional support and resources.

Family Involvement
Engage families as partners in the educational process, keeping them informed and involved in decision-making and the home application of school-based strategies.

TIC DISORDERS

WHAT ARE TIC DISORDERS?

Definition - *Tic disorders involve sudden, repetitive motor movements or vocalizations that are involuntary.*

TYPES OF TICS

Motor Tics

Examples include **blinking, shrugging**, or **facial grimacing**.

Vocal Tics

Examples include **grunting, throat clearing**, or **repeating words**.

TYPES OF TIC DISORDERS

Transient Tic Disorder
Tics last for less than one year.

Chronic Tic Disorder
Tics persist for more than one year, can be either motor or vocal.

Tourette Syndrome
Presence of both motor and vocal tics for more than one year.

Diagnosis and Impact
Diagnosis: Based on the history of symptoms and clinical observations.
Impact: Can affect academic performance, social interactions, and emotional well-being.

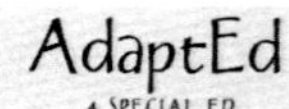

EDUCATIONAL SUPPORTS
FOR STUDENTS WITH TIC DISORDERS

ACCOMMODATIONS IN THE SCHOOL SETTING

Individualized Education Plans (IEP) or 504 Plans:

Essential for providing specific accommodations tailored to the student's needs.

In-Class Strategies:

Flexible Seating Options Allowing the student to sit where they feel most comfortable.

Breaks
Permitting the student to take breaks as needed to manage tics.

Supportive Interventions

Behavioral Therapy
Techniques such as Comprehensive Behavioral Intervention for Tics (CBIT) can be facilitated through school resources.

Counseling and Support
Access to school psychologists or counselors to address emotional or social challenges.

Teacher and Staff Education

Awareness Training Workshops or training sessions on tic disorders to educate teachers and staff about the condition and effective support strategies.

Collaboration
Encouraging teamwork between the education team, the student's family, and medical professionals to ensure a cohesive support system.

EPILEPSY

UNDERSTANDING EPILEPSY IN CHILDREN

WHAT IS EPILEPSY?

Definition - *Epilepsy is a neurological disorder marked by recurrent, unprovoked seizures.*

TYPES OF TICS

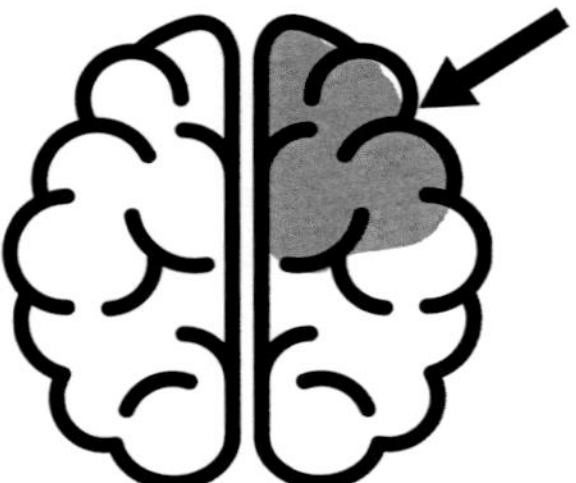

Focal Seizures

Occur in just one area of the brain.

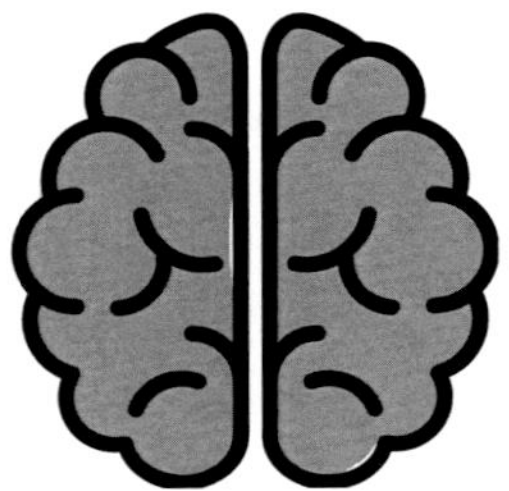

Generalized Seizures

Affect both sides of the brain.

EPIDEMIOLOGY

- Affects approximately 0.5-1% of children worldwide.
- It can begin at any age, but the highest incidence is in early childhood.

Symptoms
Vary depending on the type of seizure; may include temporary **confusion**, **staring** spells, uncontrollable **jerking movements**, and **loss of consciousness.**

Diagnosis
Typically involves **EEG (electroencephalogram)** testing, **medical history,** and sometimes **brain imaging.**

Impact on Learning and Development
Seizures can affect cognitive functions like memory and attention.
Psychological impacts include anxiety about having seizures in front of peers.

EDUCATIONAL SUPPORTS
FOR STUDENTS WITH EPILEPSY

EDUCATIONAL CHALLENGES AND ACCOMMODATIONS

Academic Needs

May require support for memory or learning gaps due to seizures or medication side effects.

Safety Considerations

Emergency protocols should be in place to manage seizures safely.

School Accommodations

Seizure Action Plan Tailored to individual needs and includes information on recognizing seizures and emergency procedures.

Inclusive Classroom Strategies

- Educating peers and staff about epilepsy to promote understanding and reduce stigma.
- Ensuring the student can participate safely in all school activities, including physical education, with appropriate modifications if necessary.

LEGAL PROTECTIONS AND RIGHTS

Individuals with Disabilities Education Act (IDEA)

Entitles students with epilepsy to an Individualized Education Plan (IEP) if their education is impacted.

Section 504 of the Rehabilitation Act

Provides protections and necessary accommodations through a 504 Plan

DOWN SYNDROME

Down syndrome is a genetic disorder caused when abnormal cell division results in an extra full or partial copy of chromosome 21. This extra genetic material causes the developmental changes and physical features of Down syndrome.

COMMON DIFFERENCES

KEY FACTS

- Varies in severity among individuals, causing lifelong intellectual disability and developmental delays.

- the most common genetic chromosomal disorder.

- commonly causes other medical abnormalities, including heart and gastrointestinal disorders.

RISK FACTORS

- Advancing maternal age.

- Being carriers of the genetic translocation for Down syndrome.

- Having had one child with Down syndrome.

EDUCATIONAL SUPPORTS
FOR STUDENTS WITH DOWN SYNDROME

INCLUSIVE EDUCATION

Integrate into Regular Classrooms

Whenever possible, include children with Down syndrome in mainstream classrooms with their peers. This integration promotes social interaction and communication skills.

Peer Supports

Use peer tutoring and cooperative learning groups to enhance social and academic skills.

DIFFERENTIATED INSTRUCTION

Tailor Learning Approaches

Customize teaching methods and materials to meet the individual needs of each child with Down syndrome.

Visual Learning

Incorporate visual aids, such as charts, pictures, and videos, which can help in understanding complex concepts.

COMMUNICATION ENHANCEMENT

Speech and Language Therapy

Integrate regular sessions to improve speech clarity and language skills.

Alternative Communication Methods

For nonverbal children or those with significant speech challenges, introduce sign language, pictures, and augmentative communication devices.

EDUCATIONAL SUPPORTS
FOR STUDENTS WITH DOWN SYNDROME

SENSORY INTEGRATION

Sensory-Friendly Environment

Create a classroom setting that considers sensory sensitivities, such as minimizing overwhelming noises and providing opportunities for physical activities.

Hands-On Learning

Engage children with Down syndrome through tactile activities that involve touching, building, or movement.

FOCUS ON LIFE SKILLS

Daily Living Activities

Incorporate training in everyday skills, such as dressing, eating, and personal hygiene, into the school curriculum.

Social Skills Development

Teach and model appropriate social behaviors through role-playing and social stories.

USE OF TECHNOLOGY

Assistive Devices

Implement technology and tools designed to support learning, such as tablets with educational apps and software that enhance reading and math skills.

Audio Books and Visuals

Utilize audiovisual materials to aid in reading comprehension and engagement.

EDUCATIONAL SUPPORTS
FOR STUDENTS WITH DOWN SYNDROME

BEHAVIORAL SUPPORT

Positive Reinforcement

Employ strategies that reinforce positive behavior, such as rewards or praise for achievements and good behavior.

Consistent Routines

Maintain a structured environment that helps children with Down syndrome feel secure and understand what to expect next.

PROFESSIONAL COLLABORATION

Team Approach

Work closely with special educators, therapists, and medical professionals to develop and implement an effective educational plan.

Parent Involvement

Actively involve parents in educational planning and decision-making. Regular communication between school and home is crucial to reinforce learning and behavioral goals.

ONGOING ASSESSMENT AND ADAPTATION

Regular Evaluation

Continuously assess educational strategies and progress, making adjustments as necessary to meet the evolving needs of the child.

Transition Planning

As children grow, plan for transitions, whether moving to new educational levels or preparing for adult life.

SENSORY PROCESSING DISORDERS

Problems processing information from the senses. This makes it hard for them to respond to that information in the right way. The senses include touch, movement, smell, taste, vision, and hearing.

Hyposensitive kids need more sensory stimulation. They often love to move around and crash into things. **Hypersensitive** kids avoid strong sensory stimulation and get overwhelmed easily.

Parents often notice first is odd behaviors and wild mood swings,
strange at best, and upsetting at worst. Usually its a
big reaction to a change in environment — a radical, inexplicable shift in the child's behavior.

Sensory processing problems are now considered a symptom of autism because the majority of children and adults on the autism spectrum also have significant sensory issues. However, many children with sensory issues are not on the spectrum. They can also be found in those with ADHD, OCD and otherdevelopmental delays — or with no otherdiagnosis at all

Occupational therapist A. Jean Ayres, PhD, identified sensory processing difficulties. In the 1970s, she proposed that some individuals struggle to process information from seven senses instead of the traditional five, impacting their ability to understand both internal and external stimuli effectively. Dr. Ayres introduced the "internal" senses of body awareness (proprioception) and movement (vestibular).

When the brain struggles to process this influx of information, it creates a metaphorical "traffic jam," where conflicting signals from various sources make it challenging to make sense of the sensory input.

Signs of sensory processing disorder include sudden mood swings and strange behavior. Kids with sensory issues might avoid bright lights or loud noises, run around crashing into things, throw tantrums, or appear clumsy.

EDUCATIONAL SUPPORTS
FOR STUDENTS WITH SENSORY PROCESSING DISORDERS

CREATE A SENSORY-FRIENDLY CLASSROOM ENVIRONMENT

Adjust Lighting and Acoustics: Use natural lighting when possible and minimize fluorescent lighting. Provide quiet spaces or noise-canceling headphones to reduce auditory distractions.

Comfortable Seating Options: Offer various seating options like stability balls, cushioned pads, or standing desks to accommodate children's needs for movement or stability.

Organized and Clutter-Free Space: Keep the classroom organized and free of unnecessary clutter to reduce visual distractions and help children focus better.

INCORPORATE SENSORY BREAKS

Scheduled Breaks

Integrate short, regular breaks for sensory activities, allowing children to reset and regulate their sensory input. This can include activities like stretching, jumping, or quiet time.

Sensory Corners

Designate a specific classroom area equipped with sensory tools such as tactile toys, stress balls, or weighted blankets that children can use to self-regulate.

USE SENSORY TOOLS AND ADAPTATIONS

Tactile Materials

Provide access to various tactile materials during lessons, such as fidget toys, play dough, or textured paper, to help maintain focus and calmness.

Visual Aids

Utilize visual schedules and organizers to help students understand and anticipate daily activities and transitions.

Auditory Supports

Use soft music or white noise machines during work to mask distracting sounds and create a calming environment.

EDUCATIONAL SUPPORTS
FOR STUDENTS WITH SENSORY PROCESSING DISORDERS

USE SENSORY TOOLS AND ADAPTATIONS

Tactile Materials

Provide access to various tactile materials during lessons, such as fidget toys, play dough, or textured paper, to help maintain focus and calmness.

Visual Aids

Utilize visual schedules and organizers to help students understand and anticipate daily activities and transitions.

Auditory Supports: Use soft music or white noise machines during work to mask distracting sounds and create a calming environment.

DIFFERENTIATED INSTRUCTIONAL TECHNIQUES

Multisensory Teaching Methods

Employ teaching methods that involve multiple senses. For example, use visual presentations, hands-on activities, and auditory storytelling to cater to sensory preferences.

Pacing and Modality

Adjust the pace of teaching and alternate between activities that require high and low levels of sensory input to accommodate different sensory thresholds.

FOSTER SOCIAL INTERACTION AND EMOTIONAL SUPPORT

Structured Social Interactions

Provide structured activities that guide children's inappropriate social behavior while considering their sensory sensitivities.

Emotional Regulation Strategies

Teach and model specific strategies for managing emotions and sensory overload, such as deep breathing techniques, visualization, or using quiet zones.

EDUCATIONAL SUPPORTS
FOR STUDENTS WITH SENSORY PROCESSING DISORDERS

COLLABORATIVE PLANNING AND SUPPORT

Collaborative Team Approach
Work closely with occupational therapists, psychologists, and parents to develop and implement educational plans tailored to the child's sensory needs.

Training for Educators
Provide training for teachers and school staff on sensory processing issues to foster a deeper understanding and better support for students.

INDIVIDUALIZED ACCOMMODATIONS

Personalized Learning Plans
Develop Individualized Education Programs (IEP) or 504 plans that specifically address sensory processing needs and outline necessary accommodations and supports.

Regular Monitoring and Adjustments
Continuously assess the effectiveness of strategies and accommodations and make adjustments based on the child's ongoing feedback and developmental changes

DEAF/HARD OF HEARING

Deaf and Hard of Hearing (DHH) students fall along a spectrum of hearing abilities, ranging from **profound deafness** (little to no hearing) to **partial hearing loss**.

TYPES OF HEARING LOSS

Conductive Hearing Loss occurs when sound is not efficiently conducted through the outer or middle ear, typically due to blockages or infections.

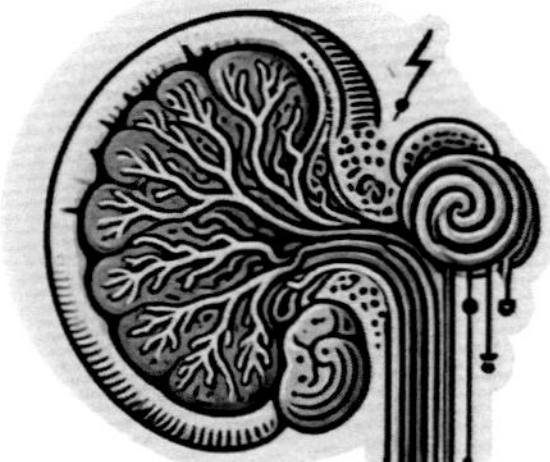

Sensorineural Hearing Loss: Results from damage to the inner ear (cochlea) or the nerve pathways to the brain. This is the most common permanent hearing loss.

Mixed Hearing Loss: A combination of both conductive and sensorineural hearing loss.

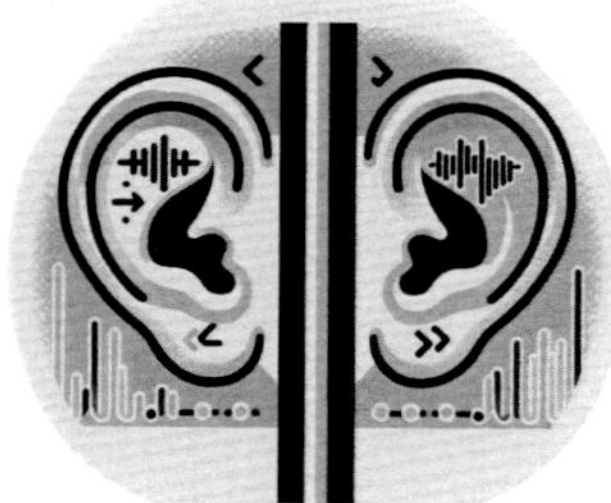

Unilateral vs. Bilateral Hearing Loss: Unilateral affects one ear, while bilateral affects both ears.

Newborn Hearing Screening: Early detection of hearing loss can lead to timely interventions.
Many states have newborn hearing screening programs that help diagnose hearing loss shortly after birth.

AdaptEd
+ SPECIAL ED

DEAF/HARD OF HEARING

American Sign Language (ASL): A visual language used primarily by the Deaf community. ASL grammar and syntax are distinct from English.

Cued Speech: A visual communication system that combines mouth movements with hand cues to help distinguish speech sounds.

Oral/Aural Communication: This type of communication focuses on using residual hearing and spoken language, often supplemented with hearing aids or cochlear implants. Even with the use of optimally programmed and functioning personal amplification, hearing will not be restored to normal level.

Total Communication (TC): A combination of communication methods (sign language, spoken language, written language, etc.) tailored to the child's needs.

Hearing Assistive Technology: Allows students to better understand speech in noisy environments. Examples could be ear level remote microphone (RM) systems or classroom sound field (CADS) systems.

SOCIAL-EMOTIONAL CONSIDERATIONS

Peer Relationships: DHH students may struggle to communicate or feel excluded from peer conversations. Educators and parents can facilitate peer interaction by teaching classmates about hearing loss and encouraging inclusive practices.

Self-Advocacy: Encouraging DHH students to express their communication needs and self-advocate in educational settings is crucial for their long-term success.

Counseling and Emotional Support: Some DHH students may benefit from counseling services to address feelings of isolation or frustration due to communication barriers.

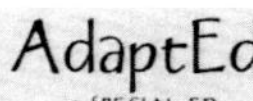

DEAF/HARD OF HEARING

Classroom Buddy: Designate a classroom peer to relay pertinent information in cases of emergencies.

Visual Supports: Use visual aids, closed captioning, and written instructions to supplement auditory information.

Strategic/Flexible Seating: Positioning D/HH students in the classroom closer to the sound source and away from background noise to help maximize their visual and auditory access.

RM Systems: A teacher wears a microphone, and the student uses a receiver, amplifying the teacher's voice directly to the student's ear.

Real-Time Captioning: Live transcription of spoken language during lectures or videos can help DHH students follow along in real-time.

Sign Language Interpreters: In cases where ASL is the primary mode of communication, a qualified sign language interpreter is essential.

Note Takers: captures essential information and, while often used in classrooms, it can be applied in any learning environment, such as job sites or internships. Deaf students particularly benefit from receiving notes from trained note-takers, as they must divide their attention between multiple accommodations—such as speech-to-text services, interpreters, captioned media—as well as the instructor, group discussions, and other presented materials.

TESTING ACCOMMODATIONS

Testing accommodations are designed to help deaf students demonstrate their knowledge by minimizing barriers related to test design, wording, and format. While accommodations vary based on individual needs, some commonly used ones include:

- **Hearing Assistive Technology**
- **Captioned Media**
- **Extended Time**
- **Glossaries or Dictionaries**
- **Individual Test Administration**
- **Frequent Breaks**
- **Sign Language Interpreters**
- **Scribes to Record Signed or Dictated Responses**

DEAF/HARD OF HEARING

HOW PARENTS AND EDUCATORS CAN COLLABORATE

Regular Communication:

Parents and educators should work together to ensure that the child's communication needs are met both at home and at school. Frequent IEP or 504 plan meetings are essential for tracking progress.

Understanding the Child's Needs:

Each DHH child is unique. Parents and/or DHH Specialist should educate teachers on the child's preferred communication method, hearing devices, and accommodations.

Community Resources:

Engage with local or national DHH organizations for support, mentorship, and advocacy. Resources like the American Society for Deaf Children or the Alexander Graham Bell Association for the Deaf and Hard of Hearing offer educational tools and support networks.

BLINDNESS AND VISUAL IMPAIRMENT (VI)

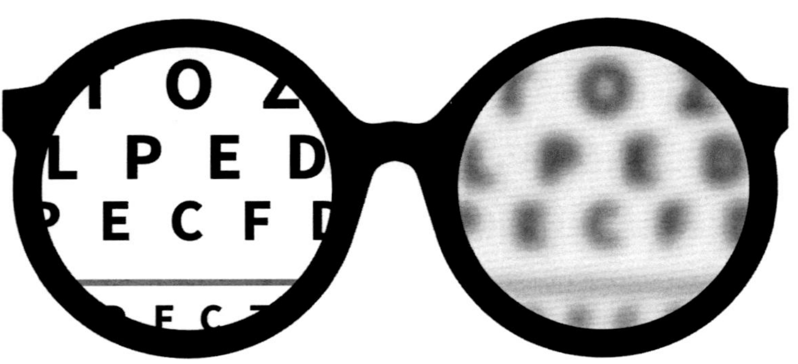

LEVELS OF VISION LOSS

Partial blindness: You still retain some vision, often referred to as "low vision."

Complete blindness: You cannot see or detect light, this condition is extremely rare.

Congenital blindness: Poor vision that is present at birth, caused by inherited eye or retinal conditions, or non-inherited birth defects.

Legal blindness: Defined by having central vision of 20/200 in the better-seeing eye, even with corrective lenses. This means you must be 10 times closer to an object or the object must be 10 times larger than for someone with 20/20 vision. It also includes having a severely reduced field of vision (less than 20 degrees).

Nutritional blindness: Vision loss due to vitamin A deficiency. Prolonged deficiency can lead to damage to the eye's surface (xerophthalmia) and may impair night vision or make it harder to see in low light because of reduced retinal function.

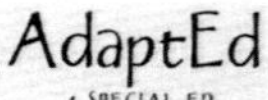

BLINDNESS AND VISUAL IMPAIRMENT (VI)

IMPACT OF VISUAL IMPAIRMENT ON LEARNING

Access to Information:
Children with visual impairments rely on alternative methods of accessing information, such as large print, magnification, Braille, auditory, tactile learning tools, and screen readers. This may impact literacy and numeracy development if not addressed early.

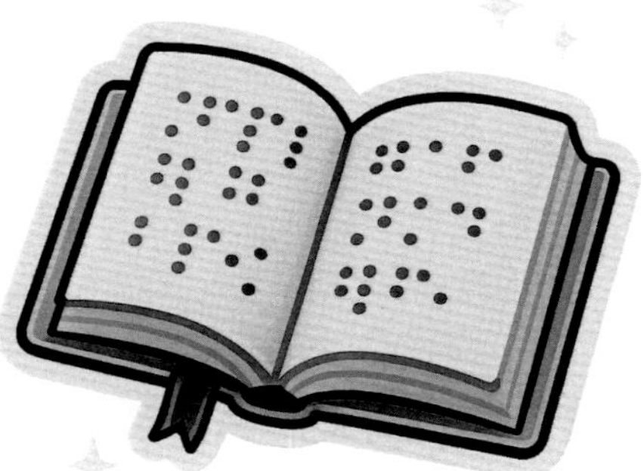

Limited ability to learn incidentally: This affects how they form concepts and develop schema or frameworks for understanding new ideas and vocabulary that provide essential foundation skills for comprehension and abstract reasoning.

Motor Development and Mobility:
Visual impairment can affect motor skills (e.g., crawling, walking) and orientation. Early intervention and mobility training, such as orientation and mobility (O&M) instruction for some students, can be crucial for independent travel and spatial awareness.

Social and Emotional Development:
Children with VI may face challenges in social interaction, understanding non-verbal cues, and forming peer relationships. Specialized instruction in social skills and inclusive environments can promote social-emotional growth.

Academic Achievement:
VI may affect a child's ability to access standard print and visual content (e.g., charts, graphs). Assistive technology and individualized instruction are often necessary to ensure equitable educational opportunities.

BLINDNESS AND VISUAL IMPAIRMENT (VI)

SUPPORTS AND ACCOMMODATIONS

Assistive Technology: Devices like screen readers, magnification tools, Braille writer, refreshable Braille displays, and audiobooks help students access digital and print information. Apps designed for accessibility can also facilitate communication, mobility, and learning.

Braille and Tactile Learning Tools: Braille literacy is a key skill for students who are blind. Specialized materials like tactile graphics, 3D models, and Braille textbooks can help students access their educational curriculum.

Orientation and Mobility (O&M) Training: Certified O&M specialists teach children how to navigate their environments safely and efficiently using tools such as canes, guide dogs, or electronic travel aids. This training can be vital for independence.

Expanded Core Curriculum (ECC): In addition to academic content, children with VI often need direct instruction in the ECC, which includes areas like independent living skills, career education, social skills, and compensatory skills (e.g., large print, Braille, auditory learning strategies).

Individualized Education Plan (IEP) or 504 Plan: These legal documents outline the accommodations and support a student with VI is entitled to receive in school. This may include preferential seating, extended time on assignments, alternative formats (e.g., Braille, large print), one-to-one aide, and VI and/or O&M services..

BLINDNESS AND VISUAL IMPAIRMENT (VI)

ROLE OF PARENTS

ADVOCACY

Parents should work closely with schools to ensure their child receives appropriate services and accommodations. Understanding rights under the Individuals with Disabilities Education Act (IDEA) and Section 504 of the Rehabilitation Act is critical.

COLLABORATION WITH PROFESSIONALS:

Parents are key members of the educational team and should collaborate with teachers, O&M specialists, vision teachers, and therapists to ensure their child's unique needs are met.

ROLE OF EDUCATORS

Inclusive Classroom Practices:
Teachers should use multimodal teaching strategies to ensure lessons are accessible to students with VI.
This may include auditory explanations, hands-on activities, and providing materials in accessible formats.

Professional Development:
Educators benefit from training in modifying the classroom environment and instructional materials for students with VI. Awareness of assistive technology and accessible learning resources is essential.

Collaboration with Specialists:
Regular communication with vision specialists and O&M instructors can help ensure students receive the correct support at the right time.

MENTAL HEALTH
DISORDERS

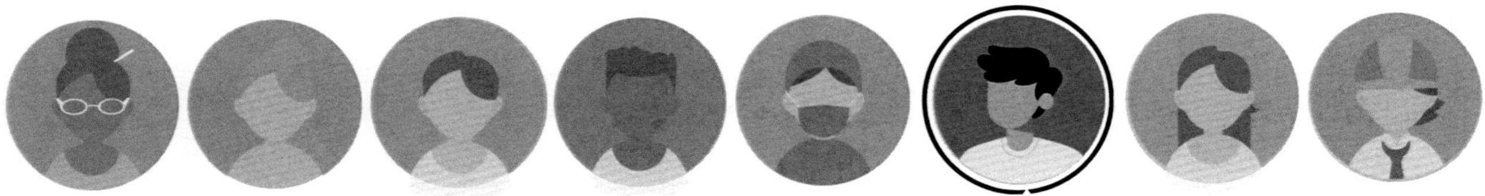

1 in every eight people in the world live with a mental health disorder

KEY FACTS

Mental disorders involve significant disturbances in...

- THINKING
- EMOTIONAL REGULATION
- OR BEHAVIOUR

There are many different types of mental disorders.

Most people do not have access to adequate care

Effective prevention and treatment options exist

A **mental disorder** involves a clinically significant disturbance in **cognition**, **emotional regulation**, or **behavior**, often leading to **distress** or **impairment** in crucial areas of functioning. These disorders encompass various types and may also be referred to as **mental health conditions**.

Despite the availability of effective prevention and treatment methods, accessibility to care remains limited for most individuals with mental disorders. Moreover, many people encounter stigma, discrimination, and violations of human rights in relation to mental health issues.

The COVID-19 pandemic in 2020 led to a significant rise in the number of individuals living with anxiety and depressive disorders.

MOST COMMON MENTAL HEALTH DISORDERS

- Anxiety
- Depression
- Bipolar Disorder
- Schizophrenia
- Disruptive Mood Dysregulation Disorder

26% anxiety increase

28% depressive disorders

Initial estimates indicate a 26% increase in anxiety and a 28% increase in major depressive disorders within just one year.

ANXIETY DISORDER

Anxiety in children is a common concern that can manifest in various forms and can be caused by a range of factors.

TYPES OF ANXIETY DISORDERS

- Generalized anxiety disorder (GAD)
- Separation anxiety disorder
- Social anxiety disorder
- Specific phobias
- Panic disorder
- Selective mutism

Causes

Anxiety in children results from g**enetic, environmental, and developmental factors.**
Genetics may predispose children to anxiety.
Environmental factors, including **family dynamics, parental modeling of anxiety behaviors, traumatic events, school pressures, and societal stressors,** also contribute significantly to childhood anxiety.

Symptoms

Symptoms of anxiety in children vary by disorder – Common symptoms include:

- Excessive worry
- Restlessness
- Irritability
- Difficulty concentrating
- Fatigue

- Muscle tension
- Difficulty sleeping
- Avoidance of certain situations.
- Physical symptoms like stomachaches or headaches.

IMPACT ON DEVELOPMENT

Untreated anxiety in children affects **social, emotional, and academic development.**
It causes difficulties in forming relationships, academic performance, and participation in activities. Untreated anxiety increases the risk of developing other mental health issues later in life.

AdaptEd
+ SPECIAL ED

ANXIETY
SCHOOL SUPPORTS

1 TEACH COPING SKILLS

Provide lessons and teach a coping skill strategies by the school psychologist or counselor.

2 PROVIDE STRUCTURED LEARNING ENVIRONMENT

Use of a predictable environment though use of a schedule and frontloading.

3 SAFE & INCLUSIVE ENVIRONMENT

The teacher supports students' needs and make them feel safe and able to express emotions.

4 FLEXIBLE ACCOMMODATIONS

Allow for extra time, on assignments, breaks, and provide an area for the student to calm down and relax.

5 PROVIDE FIDGETS

Provide Fidgets to help with calming

6 CHUNKING

Breaking larger assignments into smaller parts

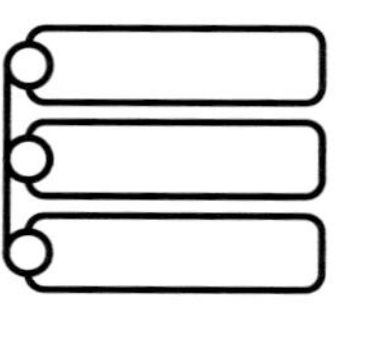

DEPRESSION

Anxiety in children is a common concern that can manifest in various forms and can be caused by a range of factors.

TYPES OF DEPRESSION

- Major Depressive Disorder (MDD)
- Persistent Depressive Disorder (PDD)
- Seasonal Affective Disorder (SAD)
- Bipolar Disorder
- Psychotic Depression
- Postpartum Depression (PPD)
- Premenstrual Dysphoric Disorder (PMDD)

Causes

Depression can be caused by a combination of genetic, biological, environmental, and psychological factors.

Symptoms

- Feelings of Worthlessness or Guilt
- Difficulty Concentrating or Making Decisions
- Agitation or Irritability
- Physical Symptoms
- Suicidal Thoughts or Behaviors
- Persistent Sadness:
- Loss of Interest or Pleasure
- Changes in Appetite or Weight
- Sleep Disturbances
- Fatigue or Loss of Energy

IMPACT ON DEVELOPMENT

- Academic Performance
- Social Relationship
- Emotional Development
- Physical Health
- Self-Esteem and Self-Concept
- Risk of Self-Harm or Suicide
- Long-Term Impact

DEPRESSION
SCHOOL SUPPORTS

1 **TEACH COPING SKILLS**
Provide lessons and teach a coping skill strategies by the school psychologist or counselor.

OFFER SUPPORT AND ENCOURAGEMENT
Look for opportunities for students to succeed in the classroom.

3 **GIVE EXTRA TIME TO COMPLETE ASSIGNMENTS**
Allow for extra time and flexibility In the classroom.

2

5

4 **MAKE PHYSICAL ACTIVITIES A PART OF YOUR DAILY CLASSROOM ROUTINE.**

MAKE BRIEF MINDFULNESS PRACTICES A PART OF EVERYDAY INSTRUCTION.

6 **SAFE AND INCLUSIVE ENVIRONMENT**
The teacher supports students' needs and make them feel safe and able to express emotions.

BIPOLAR DISORDER

Bipolar disorder is a mental health condition characterized by **significant mood swings**, including emotional highs (**mania or hypomania**) and lows (**depression**). These mood swings can affect a person's energy level, ability to concentrate, and overall behavior.

SIGNS & SYMPTOMS

Manic Phase

- Increased energy, activity, and restlessness
- Excessively "high" or euphoric mood
- Extreme irritability and distractibility
- Decreased need for sleep
- Poor judgment, planning, and impulse control
- Increased talkativeness

Depressive Phase

- Persistent sad, anxious, or "empty" mood
- Feelings of hopelessness or pessimism
- Feelings of guilt, worthlessness, or helplessness
- Decreased energy or fatigue
- Difficulty concentrating, remembering, or making decisions
- Changes in appetite or weight

IMPACT ON LEARNING

Students with bipolar disorder may experience fluctuating academic performance, inconsistent class participation, and challenges in maintaining relationships with peers and staff. During manic phases, a student may have trouble focusing and behave disruptively, while depressive phases can lead to missed school days and a lack of participation.

BIPOLAR
SCHOOL SUPPORTS

1 **SECTION 504 OR IEP**

Can provide accommodations like extra time, scheduled breaks, modified workload.

BEHAVIORAL SUPPORT

Positive behavior support plans can help manage and reduce problematic behaviors in the classroom. Clear, consistent routines and rules help minimize confusion and stress. De-escalation techniques should be known and used by staff to handle outbursts or episodes safely. **2**

3 **STAFF TRAINING**

Professional development to help staff understand these disorders and how to support students. Crisis intervention training can be valuable for safely managing acute episodes at school.

4 **MENTAL HEALTH RESOURCES**

On-site counseling services can provide immediate support during the school day and help manage crises.

ENVIRONMENTAL ADJUSTMENTS

Quiet Spaces and Sensory Tools **5**

SOCIAL SKILLS & PEER INTERACTIONS

Social Skills Training
Positive Peer Buddy **6**

DISRUPTIVE MOOD DYSREGULATION
DISORDER (DMDD)

Disruptive Mood Dysregulation Disorder is a childhood condition characterized by **severe irritability, anger, and frequent, intense temper outbursts**. DMDD goes beyond typical childhood irritability and represents a severe impairment that requires clinical attention.

It is diagnosed in children between the ages of 6 and 18, focusing on those who exhibit symptoms consistently across different settings, such as at home and at school.

SIGNS & SYMPTOMS

- Severe temper outbursts (verbal or behavioral) that are grossly out of proportion in intensity or duration to the situation.
- Outbursts occur three or more times a week.
- Mood between outbursts: Persistently irritable or angry most of the day, nearly every day, and observable by others.
- Symptoms are present for 12 or more months and do not clear for more than three consecutive months.
- Symptoms are present in at least two settings (e.g., at school and at home), and are severe in at least one of these.

IMPACT ON LEARNING STUDENTS WITH DMDD

May struggle with academic performance due to difficulty concentrating, high levels of frustration, and problems with peer interactions. These students might also resist authority, experience frequent conflicts, and have a negative self-image, which can interfere with their ability to benefit from the educational environment.

D M D D

1 CONSISTENT ROUTINES

Provide a predictable schedule and clear expectations to reduce anxiety and prevent outbursts.

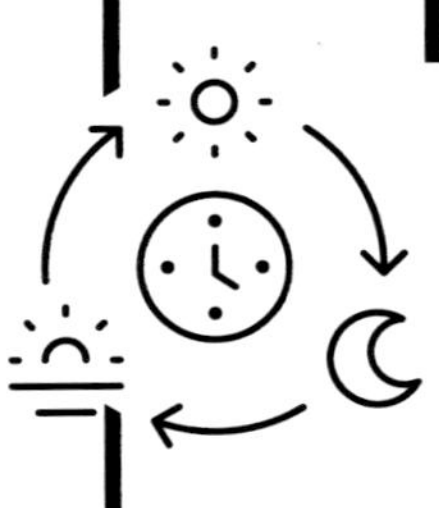

CALM ENVIRONMENT

Create a calming corner or area where the student can go to regroup and gain control.

2

3 BEHAVIOR MANAGEMENT PLANS

Work with school psychologists or counselors to implement plans that reinforce positive behaviors.

4 EMPATHETIC COMMUNICATION

Approach the student with understanding and patience, especially during moments of frustration or anger.

5 SKILL BUILDING

each and reinforce skills for emotion regulation, such as deep breathing, identifying emotions, and positive self-talk.

6 PARENT PARTNERSHIP

Maintain open communication with parents to share strategies and monitor progress.

STRATEGIES

for Managing
Specific Challenges

EDUCATIONAL STRATEGIES

There are thousands of educational strategies available with just a simple Google search. Here are a few based on the person's deficit that may be useful.

VISUAL PERCEPTUAL DEFICITS

PRESENTING PROBLEM:

Reverses or inverts letters or numerals

INTERVENTIONS

1.) **Visual Strip of letters and numbers** on the desk for students to refer to throughout the day.

2.) Trace letters in **different mediums:** for example, have the child trace the letter they are struggling with at least ten times each day in sand, in Play-Doh, using chalk, etc.; this will build muscle memory.

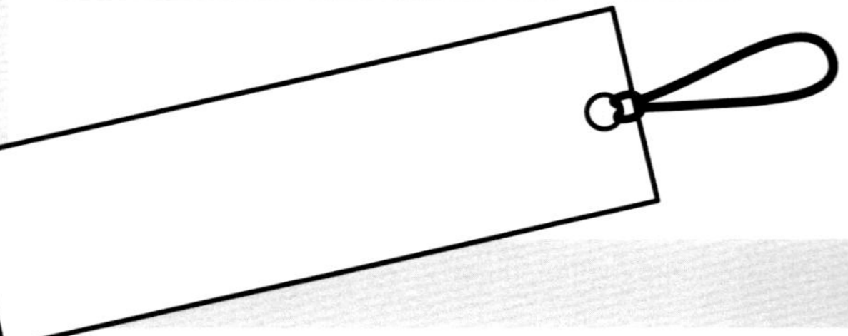

PRESENTING PROBLEM:

Loses place, skips lines, omits words and re-reads lines

INTERVENTIONS

1.) **Use a bookmark to follow line by line.** The best bookmarks are about six inches long and one inch wide, with a one-inch dark line in the center. This dark line is placed under the word the child reads as they move the marker from left to right.

2.) **Make a copy of the text** and have the person underline as they read

VISUAL PERCEPTUAL DEFICITS

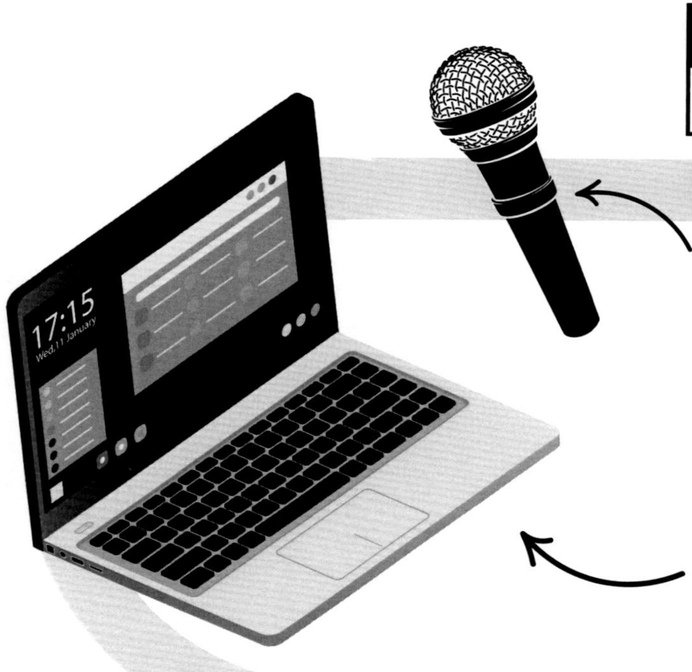

PRESENTING PROBLEM:

Slow, laborious handwriting.

INTERVENTIONS

1.) Allow **oral responses**

2.) **Shortened Assignments**

3.) Use **assistive technology** such as a computer or assistive apps (Co-Writer/Grammarly/Google Read and Write/Snap and Read)

PRESENTING PROBLEM:

Lining up math problems

INTERVENTION

1) **Graph paper** — Depending on the age, you can create different-sized graph paper boxes (several blank pages are available with a simple internet search).

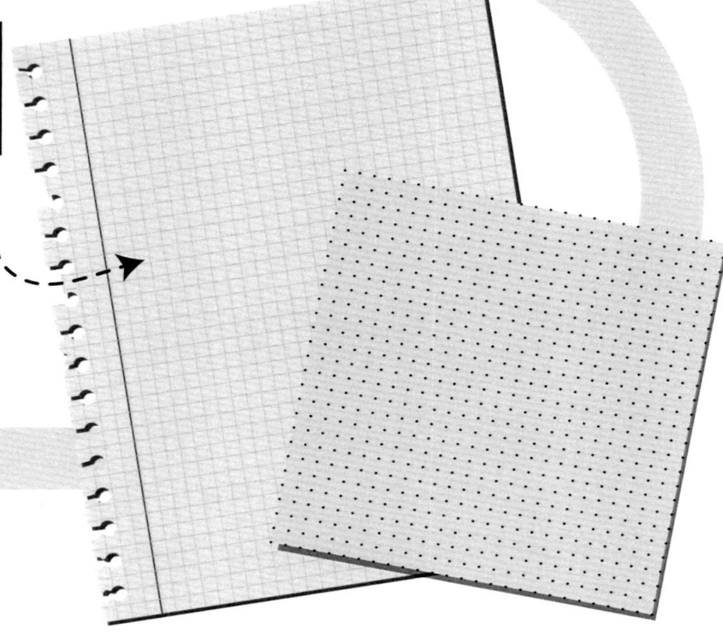

EDUCATIONAL STRATEGIES

AUDITORY PROCESSING DEFICITS

PRESENTING PROBLEM:

Cannot understand conversation delivered at a normal speed (This may be evidenced by the student's " Huh? " or " What? ")

INTERVENTIONS

1) **Seating**

Place the person near the speaker to reduce distractions and improve access to speech.

2) <u>**Speaking**</u>

Speak slowly and clearly, and use a slightly lower volume. Avoid asking students to listen and write at the same time.

Instructions

- Give clear, step-by-step instructions in short sentences, and emphasize keywords.
- Use logical sequencing words like "first," "next," and "finally". Repeat key information and rephrase as needed.
- Check for understanding by asking students to summarize or repeat what you said.

3) **Visual aids**

Use visual tools, images, and gestures to support spoken lessons. For example, you can pre-teach new words or use visual cues.

AdaptEd
4 SPECIAL ED

EDUCATIONAL STRATEGIES

AUDITORY PROCESSING DEFICITS

PRESENTING PROBLEM:

Unable to filter out extraneous noises.

INTERVENTIONS

1) **Place near a positive peer** who can repeat the information as needed

2) **Simplify directions.**

3) **Teach a person to advocate for oneself** when needing information repeated or restated.

4) **Provide a handout** of key points during the lecture.

5) **Test in a quiet environment** or separate space.

6) **Provide a speaker with a mic and amplification** throughout the room.

MEMORY DEFICITS

PRESENTING PROBLEM:

Cannot remember what they just saw.

INTERVENTIONS

1) **Play memory games**, such as showing ten objects for 30 seconds, and then have the person try to recall what they saw.

2) **Teach note-taking skills.**

3) **Allow open-book tests.**

4) **Teach mnemonic devices.**

TYPES OF
MNEMONIC DEVICES

- Acronyms & Acrostics
- Method of Loci
- Songs & Rhymes
- Chunking
- Association

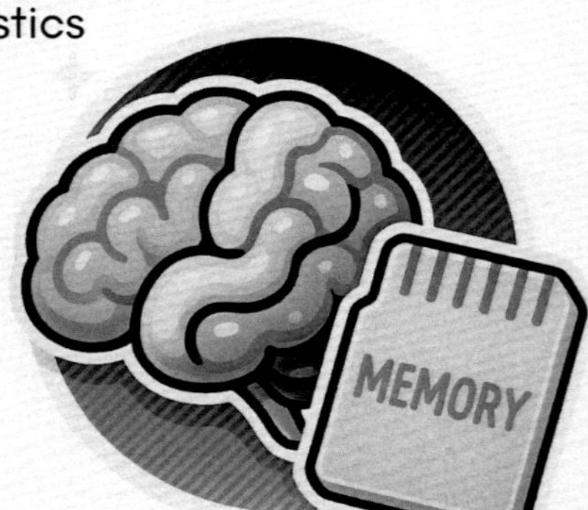

PRESENTING PROBLEM:

Cannot remember what they saw or heard

INTERVENTIONS

1) **Weed out** nonessential information.

2) **Repetition.**

3) **Presume competence.**

4) **Allow Calculators.**

5) **Concrete examples:** see, hear, and then do.

BEHAVIOURAL STRATEGIES

Behavioral strategies for people with disabilities can be highly effective in promoting positive outcomes and improving quality of life. These strategies are often **tailored to individual needs** and can vary widely depending on the **type and severity of the disability.**

POSITIVE REINFORCEMENT

Definition: Rewarding desired behaviors to increase the likelihood of their recurrence.

Examples: Verbal praise, tangible rewards (stickers, tokens), and privileges (extra playtime)

VISUAL SUPPORTS

Definition: Using visual aids to enhance understanding and communication.
Examples: Picture schedules, social stories, and visual timers.

TASK ANALYSIS

Definition: Breaking down complex tasks into smaller, manageable steps.
Application: Teaching self-care skills, academic tasks, or job-related activities.

ENVIRONMENTAL MODIFICATIONS

Focus: Adapting the environment to reduce barriers and support positive behavior.
Examples: Adjusting lighting, reducing noise, and providing accessible materials.

PROMPTING AND FADING

Prompting: Providing cues to encourage a desired behavior.
Fading: Gradually reducing prompts as the individual gains independence.

SELF-MONITORING

Definition: Teaching individuals to track their own behavior and progress.
Tools: Checklists, journals, or digital apps.

FUNCTIONAL BEHAVIOR ASSESSMENT (FBA)

Purpose: Identifying the reasons behind challenging behaviors.
Outcome: Developing intervention plans that address the root causes of behaviors.

SOCIAL SKILLS TRAINING

Focus:Teaching appropriate social interactions and communication skills.
Methods: Role-playing, modeling, and social stories.

BEHAVIOURAL STRATEGIES

TECHNOLOGY-ASSISTED INTERVENTIONS

Tools: Apps, software, and devices designed to support learning and communication.

Examples: Speech-generating devices, educational apps, and virtual reality for social skills training.

SOCIAL STORIES AND SCRIPTS

Purpose: Preparing individuals for new or challenging situations.

Content: Short narratives or scripts that explain what to expect and how to behave.

PEER-MEDIATED INTERVENTIONS

Involvement: Engaging peers in supporting individuals with disabilities.

Benefits: Enhancing social interactions and inclusion.

INDIVIDUALIZED EDUCATION PLANS (IEPS) AND BEHAVIOR INTERVENTION PLANS (BIPS)

IEPs: Tailored educational programs for students with disabilities.

BIPs: Specific plans to address challenging behaviors in educational settings.

PARENT AND CAREGIVER TRAINING

Importance: Ensuring consistency and reinforcement of strategies across environments.

Content: Teaching effective behavior management techniques and communication strategies.

COGNITIVE BEHAVIORAL THERAPY (CBT)

Focus: Addressing thoughts and feelings that influence behavior.

Techniques: Identifying negative thought patterns and developing coping strategies.

MINDFULNESS AND RELAXATION TECHNIQUES

Goal: Reducing stress and anxiety.

Practices: Deep breathing exercises, guided imagery and mindfulness meditation.

POSITIVE REINFORCEMENT

Social Reinforcer

A child helps their parent with the dishes. The parent offers the child praise and affection for their help.

Social Reinforcer

A child starts behaving more kindly at school. Realizing this, the other students start being kinder towards them as well.

A teacher uses a sticker chart system. Students receive stickers for completing their homework, which can be exchanged for physical rewards.

Token Reinforcer

Tangible Reinforcer

You take yourself out for a sweet treat every time you're able to complete a jog.

Natural Reinforcer

You're consistent with therapy for six months and start feeling better emotionally.

You work hard and go above and beyond for one year. Your boss gives you a raise.

Tangible Reinforcer

FOOD
like candy and chips

SOUNDS
like music and funny voices

ACTIONS
like tickles and a high-five

ACTIVITIES
like dancing and jumping

INTERNAL FEELINGS
like learning a skill and meeting a goal

POSITIVE REINFORCEMENT
LOOKS DIFFERENT FOR EVERYONE!

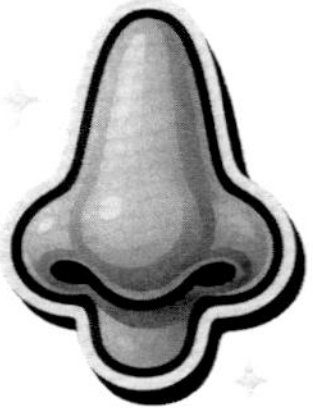

COMPLIMENTS
like "Good job!" and You did it!"

SCENTS
like coffee and lotion

DRINKS
like soda and milkshake

ITEMS
like stickers & electronics

PEOPLE
like peers and family

TASK ANALYSIS

Task Analysis (TA) consists of six steps...

1 Identifying the Target Skill.

2 Identifying the prerequisite skills of the learner and the materials needed to teach the task.

3 Breaking the skill into components.

4 Confirming that the task is completely analyzed.

5 Determining how the skill will be taught.

6 Implementing intervention and monitoring progress.

ACTUAL EXAMPLE:

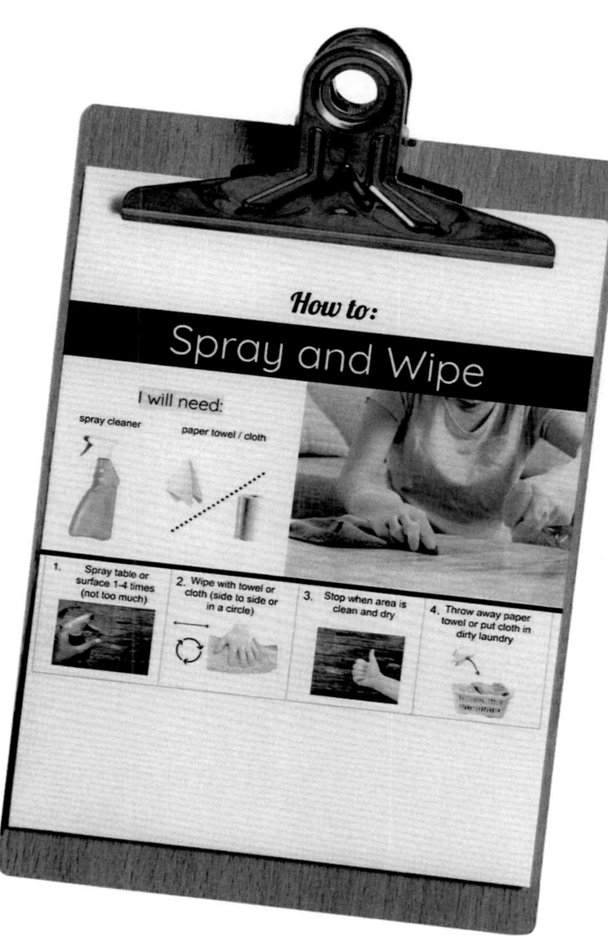

VISUAL SUPPORTS

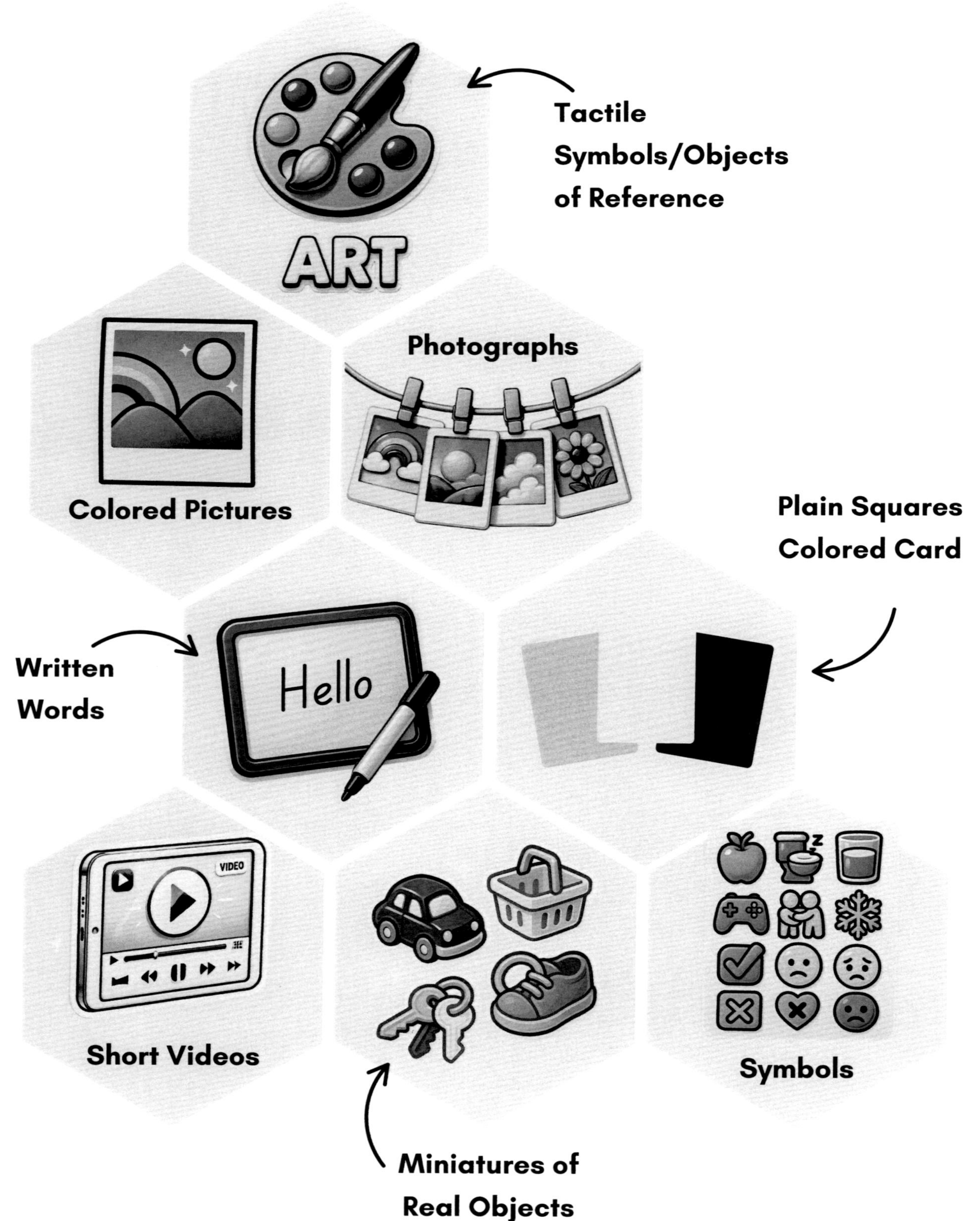

SOCIAL SKILLS TRAINING

THE STEPS OF SOCIAL SKILLS TRAINING

Step 1: Rationale

Provide reasons why it is important for your client to learn the skill.

Step 2: Steps

Break the skill down into manageable steps.

Step 3: Demonstration

Modeling the skill to your client.

Step 4: Role Play

Encourage your client to participate in a role-play using the skill. In groups, clients can role-play with each other.

Step 5: Feedback

Talk with your client about how it went. Be sure to include praise and suggestions for improvement.

Step 6: Practice

Encourage your client to practice the skill outside of the session in real-life situations.

STRATEGIES FOR TEACHING SOCIAL SKILLS

Create social scripts binder.

Integrate art activities.

Use literature.

Model and practice together.

Use social skills writing prompts.

Practice social problem-solving.

Play games and sports.

FUNCTIONAL BEHAVIOR ASSESSMENT
(FBA)

STEPS OF THE BASIC FBA

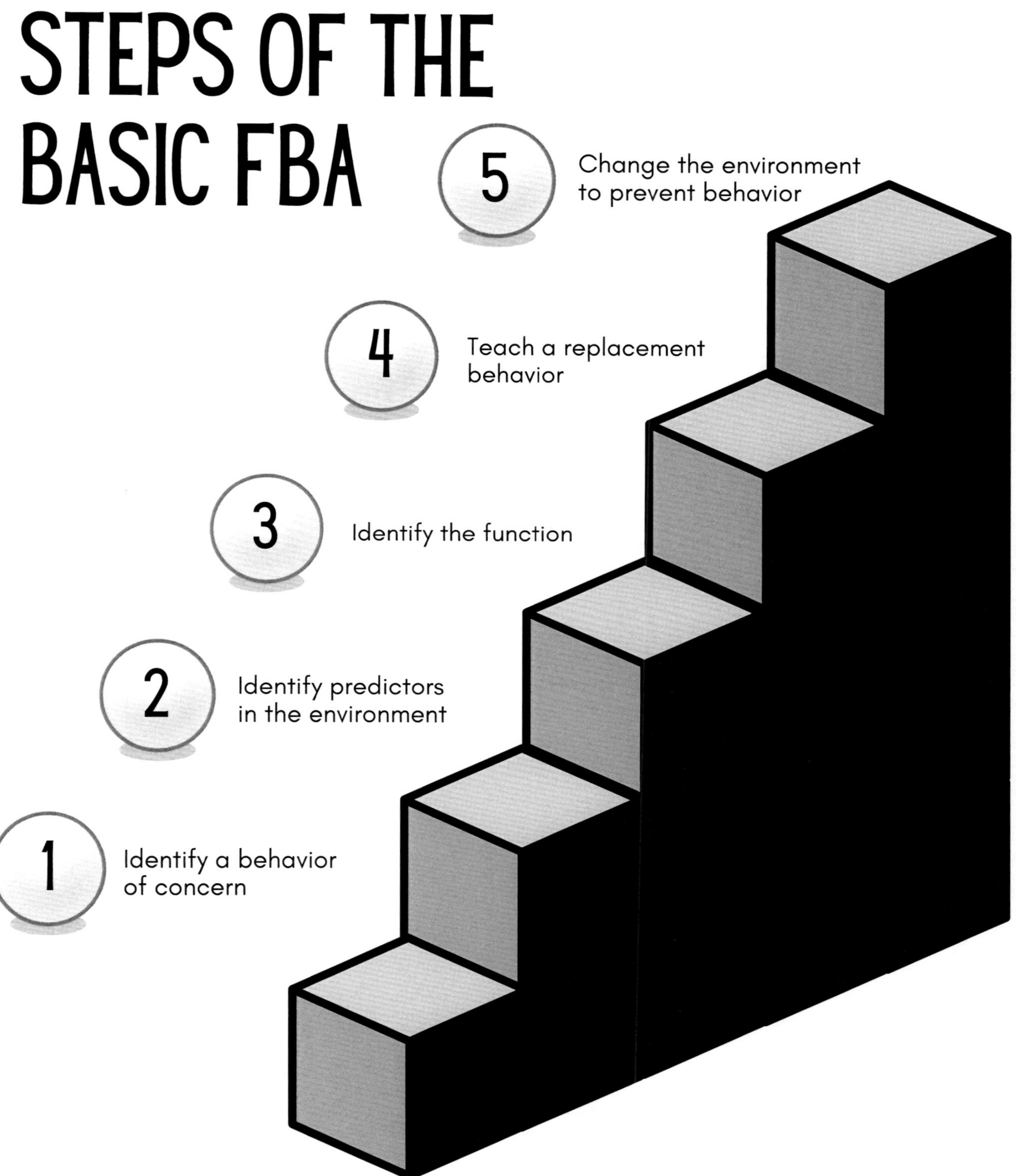

SELF-MONITORING

Self-Monitoring Log

Name: Jasmine Week of: 10/17

Target Behaviors	M	T	W	TH	F	Total
Raise hand	✓	✓	–	✓	–	3
Ignore others	✓	✓	✓	✓	✓	5
Remain seated	✓	✓	✓	–	–	3

Comments:

I forgot to take my pill on Friday because I woke up late.

Friday Report

Name: Jasmine Date: 10-21

Target Behaviors	Total
Raise hand	3/5
Ignore others	5/5
Remain seated	3/5
Total Points Possible:	11/15

Comments:

Jasmine is working hard to ignore others' inappropriate actions. She continues to need reminders to raise her hand.

Parent / Guardian Signature

EXAMPLES OF STRATEGIES

SELF-MONITORING

Troubleshooting: The teacher could have a separate copy of the sheet and circle the number on her sheet, and the students circle the number on their sheet and then compare.

STEP 1

Identify the target behavior and type it in the box.

STEP 2

Identify the target number of matches.

After each time, the teacher and the student will rate the student's behavior and circle the appropriate number and if the numbers match by circling yes or no.

Allow the student to circle the number first.

STEP 3

At the end of the day, total the number of matches and enter the number at the bottom.

If the student meets their target match goal, you can incorporate a reward menu for reinforcement.

STEP 4

You can also enter the total number of points at the bottom of the sheet, which can be incorporated into a target goal.

For example, in addition to meeting the total number of target behavior matches, you can also set a point goal for the student each day.

TIP: You will need the student's "buy-in" to effectively implement this intervention. Consider incorporating a reward system or reward menu into this intervention. The last page of this product shows an example of a reward menu that can be used.

EXAMPLES OF STRATEGIES

SELF-MONITORING

TARGET GOAL : "I WILL KEEP RAISING MY HAND TO SHARE IN CLASS."
TARGET NUMBER OF MATCHES : 4 (A POSSIBILITY OF 6 IN THIS CHART)

1 = Did not meet the behavior | 2 = Needs improvement | 3= Great Work

Subject Area/ Time of the Day	Teacher Rating (Circle only one)	Student Rating (Circle only one)	Do they match? (Circle only one)
Seatwork	1 (2) 3	1 (2) 3	(Yes) No
ELA	1 2 (3)	1 2 (3)	(Yes) No
Recess	1 (2) 3	1 2 (3)	Yes (No)
Math	1 2 (3)	1 2 (3)	(Yes) No
Lunch	1 (2) 3	1 (2) 3	(Yes) No
End of Day Activities	(1) 2 3	1 2 (3)	Yes (No)
Total Number	**13**	**16**	No. of matches = **4**

EXAMPLES OF STRATEGIES

Eliminating large open spaces where children feel overwhelmed or will run. In all age groups, furniture should be used to help define spaces and encourage safe traffic patterns

Take into consideration how **light, temperature, and noise** may influence a person's behaviors.

Provide clearly defined spaces for:

LEARNING

PLAY

PERSONAL NEEDS

Provide adequate materials
There should be sufficient materials to provide children with a variety of choices each day.

EXAMPLES OF STRATEGIES

PROMPTING AND FADING

MOST RESTRICTIVE TO LEAST RESTRICTIVE

Gestural
Point or Nod

Visual (Full and Partial)
Picture Prompt

Verbal (Full and Partial)
Say or Tell

Model (Full and Partial)
Show the action

Physical (Full and Partial)
Show the person using hand over hand or guiding hand

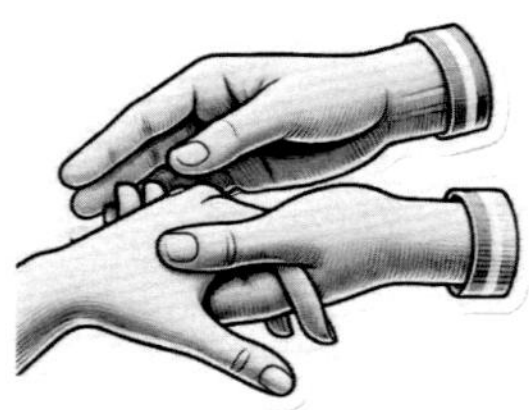

AdaptEd
4 SPECIAL ED

EXAMPLES OF STRATEGIES

PEER-MEDIATED INTERVENTIONS

PMI, a teacher trains peers to provide support in a variety of ways, including:

MODELING

Peers demonstrate appropriate behaviors or skills, such as how to initiate social interactions

PROMPTING

Peers ask questions to help students, such as "What do you do next?" or "What materials do you need?"

REINFORCEMENT

Peers reinforce targeted behavioral outcomes

OBSERVING

Peers learn from each other.

PMI can also include cooperative learning strategies. For example, a teacher might seat a trained peer next to a student with ASD during a group activity to encourage social interactions. The peer could ask the student to pass materials or help with a task.

Studies have found that PMI can be a practical approach to helping students with ASD improve their social skills, such as social communication, social responses, and social initiations.

EXAMPLES OF STRATEGIES

COGNITIVE BEHAVIORAL THERAPY

Cognitive behavioral therapy (CBT) is a collaborative process between a therapist and patient to develop skills to modify thinking, beliefs, and responses. CBT techniques can vary depending on the issue being treated, but some common examples include:

JOURNALING

Recording thoughts and emotions, including negative and positive ones. A gratitude journal can help express appreciation for positive experiences.

EXPOSURE

Exposing yourself to situations that cause anxiety, such as a crowded public space.

ROLE-PLAYING

Taking on different characters to embody situations and develop skills. This can be used to prepare for interactions with others.

SKILLS TRAINING

Learning new skills, such as communication, social, or assertiveness skills. This can also include improving self-talk.

ASSISTIVE TECHNOLOGIES AND TOOLS

Assistive technology consists of devices and services. An assistive technology device is an item or piece of equipment that helps a person with a disability increase, maintain, or improve a student's functional capabilities. Assistive technology devices can be high-tech or low-tech.

EXAMPLES OF ASSISTIVE TECHNOLOGY DEVICES

Wheelchair or wheelchair ramp

Voice-activated computer

Electronic note takers

Large-print books

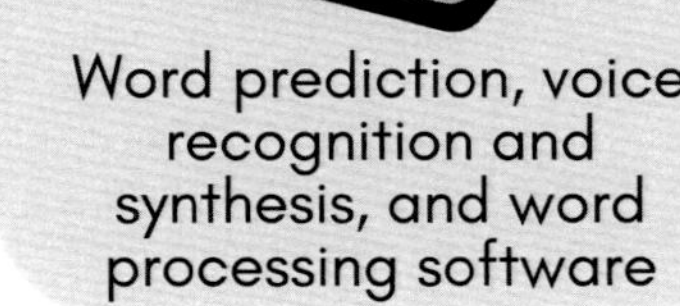

Word prediction, voice recognition and synthesis, and word processing software

Switches and controls for access to equipment

Braille flashcards/ pegboards

Pencil grips

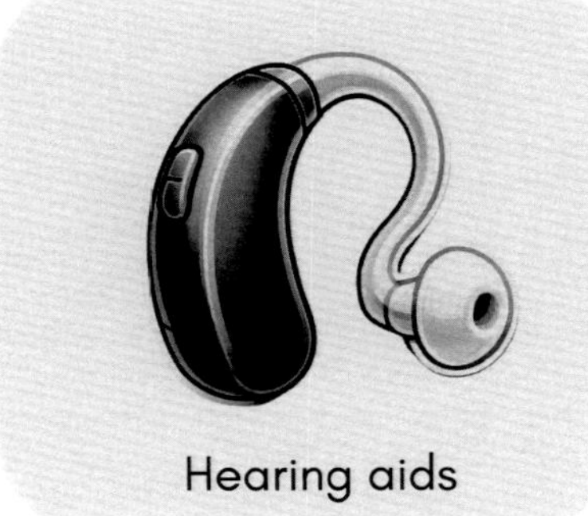

Hearing aids

Medical devices that are surgically implanted are not considered assistive technology devices.

ASSISTIVE TECHNOLOGIES AND TOOLS

An assistive technology service is any direct assistance to the student with a disability in selecting, acquiring, or using the assistive technology device. Assistive technology services include, but are not limited to:

- an evaluation of a student's need, including a functional assessment in the student's customary environment
- the purchasing, leasing, or acquiring of an assistive technology device;
- the selection, design, fitting, adapting, repairing, and replacing of an assistive technology device; and
- The training or technical assistance for a student, the student's family, or other professionals who provide services to or are otherwise substantially involved in the student's primary life functions.

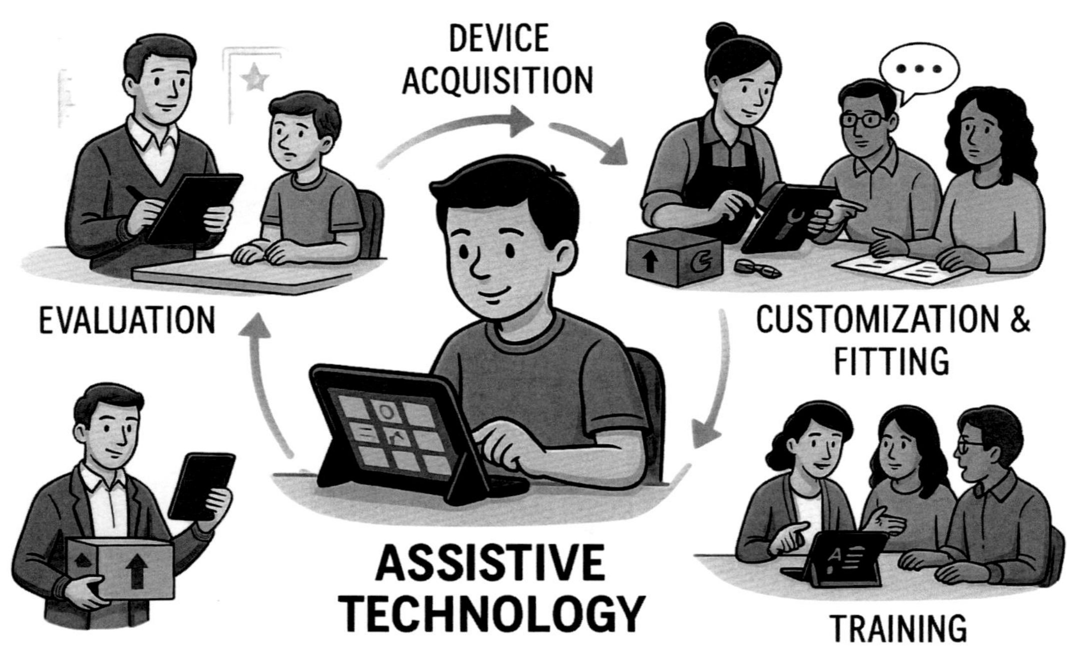

SOCIAL INCLUSION PROGRAMS

Community Centers

Establishing centers that offer various activities and services, such as educational workshops, recreational activities, and social events, to bring people together.

Inclusive Education

Promoting an educational system that accommodates all students, including those with disabilities, ensures equal learning and participation opportunities.

Employment Programs

Creating job training and placement programs that target marginalized groups, helping them gain employment and economic independence.

Cultural Competency Training

Educating community members and service providers about the diverse cultural backgrounds of the community to promote understanding and inclusion.

Language and Literacy Programs

Language classes and literacy programs are offered to help non-native speakers and those with limited literacy skills communicate and integrate better into the community.

EMOTIONAL SUPPORT
AND MENTAL HEALTH INTERVENTIONS

COMMUNITY SUPPORT PROGRAMS

Support Groups: Facilitating support groups for various needs, such as mental health, addiction recovery, parenting, and grief, where individuals can share experiences and support each other.

Volunteer Programs: Encouraging community members to volunteer their time and skills to support local initiatives, fostering a sense of community and mutual aid.

Health and Wellness Programs: Providing access to healthcare services, mental health counseling, fitness activities, and nutritional education to promote overall well-being.

Neighborhood Watch Programs: Organizing community-led initiatives to enhance safety and security in local areas, encouraging residents to look out for each other.

Housing Assistance: Offering support for individuals and families facing housing insecurity through subsidized housing, rental assistance, and homeless shelters.

EMOTIONAL SUPPORT
AND MENTAL HEALTH INTERVENTIONS

IMPLEMENTATION STRATEGIES

Partnerships with Local Organizations: Collaborating with non-profits, local businesses, and government agencies to pool resources and expertise.

Community Engagement: Actively involving community members in the planning and implementation of programs to ensure they meet the actual needs and preferences of the community.

Accessible Services: Ensuring that programs and services are accessible to all, including those with disabilities, by providing necessary accommodations.

Monitoring and Evaluation: Regularly assess the effectiveness of programs and make adjustments based on feedback and changing needs.

Funding and Resources: Securing funding from various sources, such as government grants, private donations, and fundraising events, to sustain and expand programs.

CHALLENGES AND CONSIDERATIONS

Addressing Barriers: Identifying and addressing barriers to participation, such as transportation issues, financial constraints, or language barriers.

Cultural Sensitivity: Ensuring that programs are culturally sensitive and respectful of the diverse backgrounds of community members.
Sustainability: Developing strategies to ensure the long-term sustainability of programs, including securing ongoing funding and community support.

Building Trust: Establishing trust within the community, particularly among marginalized groups who may have experienced discrimination or exclusion in the past.

By implementing these programs, communities can create a more inclusive and supportive environment, enhancing the quality of life for all residents and fostering a stronger, more cohesive society.

STRATEGIES FOR DATA COLLECTION

Data collection in special education is crucial for monitoring student progress, informing individualized education plans (IEPs), and ensuring that students receive appropriate support and accommodations. Here are the primary types of data collected in schools for special education:

TYPES OF DATA COLLECTION

ACADEMIC PERFORMANCE DATA

Standardized Tests: Scores from state and national standardized tests to assess academic achievement and compare progress with peers.
Formative Assessments: Ongoing assessments such as quizzes, classroom assignments, and teacher-made tests to monitor learning in real-time.
Summative Assessments: End-of-unit or term tests and projects that evaluate cumulative knowledge.
Curriculum-Based Measurements (CBM): Regular assessments aligned with the curriculum to track progress in core academic areas like reading, math, and writing.

BEHAVIORAL DATA

Frequency Counts: Tracking the number of times a specific behavior occurs within a set period.
Duration Recording: Measuring how long a behavior lasts.
Interval Recording: Observing whether a behavior occurs or does not occur during specified intervals.
Behavior Rating Scales: Using standardized tools to rate the severity or frequency of behaviors.
Antecedent-Behavior-Consequence (ABC) Analysis: Identifying the events that precede and follow a behavior to understand its function and develop intervention strategies.

SOCIAL-EMOTIONAL DATA

Surveys and Questionnaires: Collecting data on students' social-emotional skills, mental health, and well-being.
Observations: Documenting social interactions and emotional responses in various settings.
Counseling Records: Tracking sessions and progress in individual or group counseling.

IEP PROGRESS MONITORING

Goal Achievement: Measuring progress toward specific IEP goals and objectives.
Annual Reviews: Reviewing and updating IEPs annually based on progress data and re-evaluations.
Progress Reports: Providing regular updates to parents and guardians on their child's progress.

STRATEGIES FOR DATA COLLECTION

METHODS OF DATA COLLECTION

Direct Observation

Teachers, aides, and specialists observe and record student behaviors, academic performance, and social interactions in various settings (classroom, playground, etc.).

Standardized Testing

Administering norm-referenced tests to assess academic skills and compare them to typical developmental benchmarks.

Checklists and Rating Scales

Using standardized checklists and scales to rate skills, behaviors, and competencies. Interviews and Surveys

Conducting structured or semi-structured interviews and surveys with students, parents, and teachers to gather qualitative data.

Work Samples and Portfolios

Collecting student work samples over time to assess progress and areas needing improvement.

Digital Tools and Software

Utilizing educational software and apps to collect data on student performance and engagement with digital learning activities.

STRATEGIES FOR DATA COLLECTION

BEST PRACTICES FOR DATA COLLECTION IN SPECIAL EDUCATION

Individualization

Tailor data collection methods and tools to each student's individual needs and goals.

Consistency and Reliability

Ensure that data collection is consistent and reliable by training staff and using standardized procedures.

Confidentiality and Privacy

Adhere to legal and ethical guidelines for maintaining the confidentiality and privacy of student data, such as FERPA regulations.

Collaboration

Involve all stakeholders, including teachers, parents, specialists, and students, in the data collection process.

Data-Driven Decision Making

Use collected data to inform instructional strategies, interventions, and modifications to IEPs and BIPs.

Regular Monitoring and Reporting

Regularly monitor progress and provide timely updates to parents and other stakeholders through progress reports and meetings.

FREQUENCY COUNTS SAMPLE

Tracking the number of times a specific behavior occurs within a set period.

Student Name: JOE SMOE
Targeted Behavior: Shouting out instead of raising hand
Time Sampling period of time: 15 minutes

Date	Start Time	End Time	Classroom Activity	1	2	3	4	5	6	7	8	9	10
9/22	9:00	9:15	ELA Story	✓	✓	✓	✓	✓	✓				
9/22	11:45	12:00	Math Lecture	✓	✓	✓							
9/23	9:00	9:15	ELA Story	✓	✓	✓	✓	✓	✓	✓	✓	✓	✓
				✓	✓	✓	✓						
09/23	11:42	11:57	Math Lecture	✓									

FREQUENCY COUNTS SAMPLE

Tracking the number of times a specific behavior occurs within a set period.

Student Name:

Targeted Behavior:

Time Sampling period of time:

Date	Start Time	End Time	Classroom Activity	1	2	3	4	5	6	7	8	9	10

DURATION RECORDING SAMPLE

Measuring how long a behavior lasts.

Student Name: Patrick Starfish
Setting: 2nd grade special day class mod/sev
Definition of Behavior: Student has tantrums, showing signs of anger (clenched fists, yelling, cursing, kicking, refusal to follow directions, punching or using obscene gestures)

Date	Start Time	End Time	Duration
02/18/24	8:45 am	9:22 am	37 minutes
	12:17 pm	1:05 pm	48 minutes
02/19/24	10:22 am	10:35 am	13 minutes

DURATION RECORDING SAMPLE

Measuring how long a behavior lasts.

Student Name:

Setting:

Definition of Behavior:

Date	Start Time	End Time	Duration

ABC DATA SHEET SAMPLE

Identifying the events that precede and follow a behavior to understand its function and develop intervention strategies.

Student Name: ___________________________

Setting Event	Antecedent (A)	Behavior (B)	Consequence (C)
In Math Class	Teacher asks students to begin quiz	Johnny yells "I hate you," and crawls under desk	Teacher sends quiz home for homework
Recess on playground	Peer takes soccer ball from bin	Jacob grabs soccer ball out of peers hands and runs away	Jacob has to sit out the rest of recess
Social Science Class	Nora I s put I nto a group to work on a project	Nora hits another peer	Nora is removed from the group
Home	Brother is playing with Jasmines favorite toy	Jasmine grabs toy out of brothers hands and hits him	Jasmine starts playing with toy

AdaptEd
4 SPECIAL ED

ABC DATA SHEET

Identifying the events that precede and follow a behavior to understand its function and develop intervention strategies.

Student Name: ____

Setting Event	Antecedent (A)	Behavior (B)	Consequence (C)

NAVIGATING THE
SCHOOL SYSTEM

CHAIN OF COMMAND

Schools can be confusing when determining whom you should go to when there is an issue and/or understanding your day-to-day role in the school system.
This sample chain of command will hopefully help you when needing support.

PARENTS CHAIN OF COMMAND

Parent
Steps to take to resolve an issue

Teacher
Your first step is to contact the teacher and try to address the issue with the teacher. If you are unable to resolve it, go to the next chain above.

1

Vice Principal or Principal
The next step is to contact the vice principal or principal and try to address the issue with the site administration. If you cannot resolve it, go to the next chain above.

2

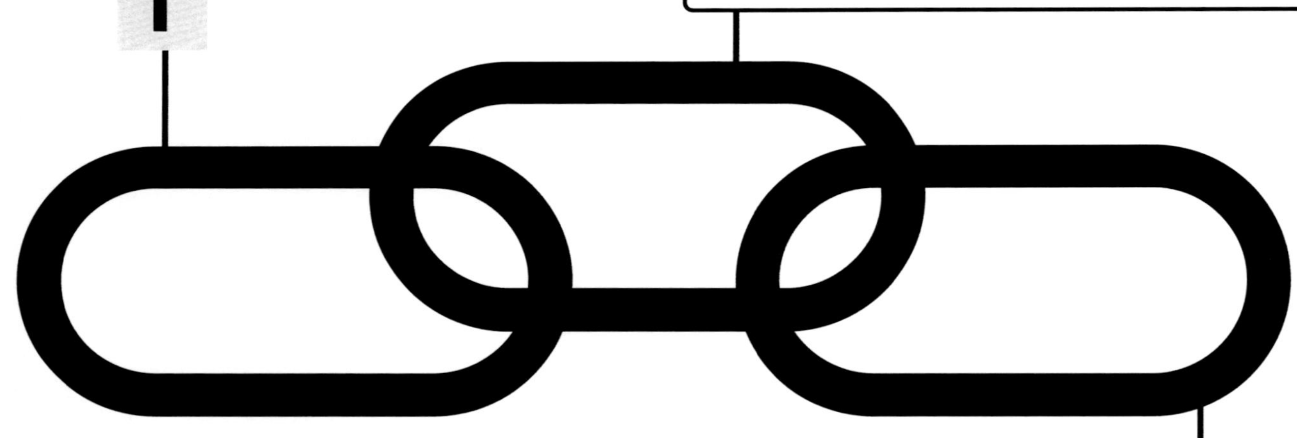

District Office/Superintendent's Office
The Final Step Is to contact the district office or superintendents office. In larger school districts there may be additional district office administration they will direct you too before going to the school board.

3

CHAIN OF COMMAND

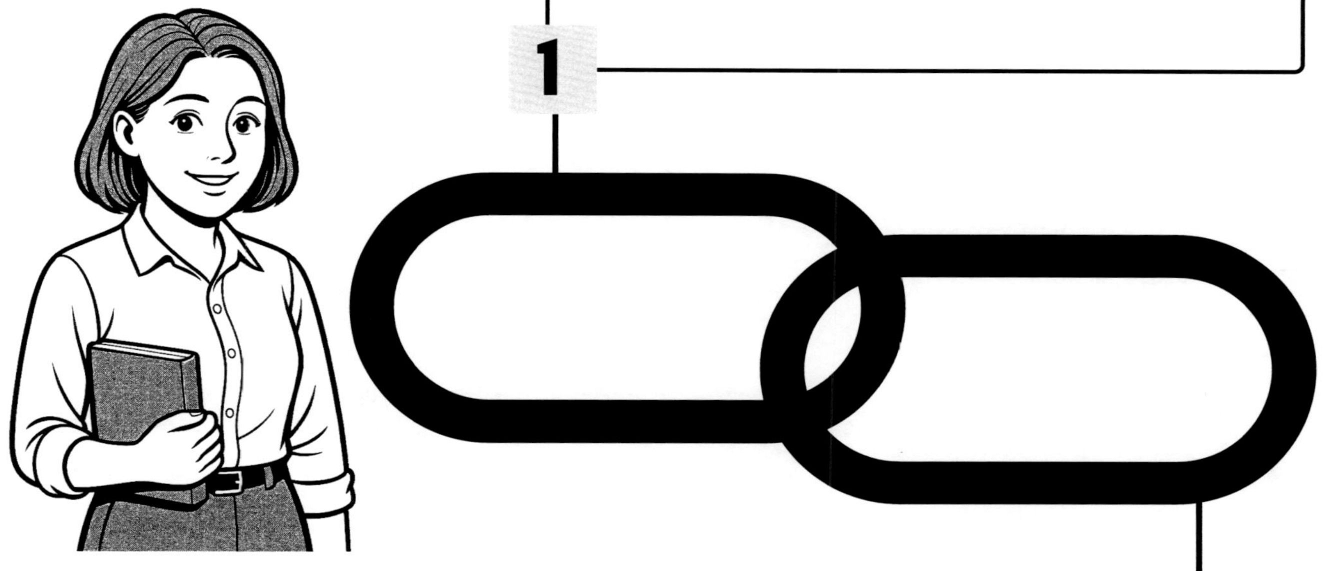

Teacher

Steps to take to resolve an issue

Vice Principal or Principal

Your first step is to meet with your site supervisor. Depending on the size of your school, that may entail a vice principal or a principal. If you have a vice principal and principal, exhaust those people before appealing to the district office.

1

Union Representative

If your Issue is unable to be resolved your next best move is to contact your teacher union site representative. Every school site typically has a representative that can connect you with the appropriate people and advise on next steps

2

CHAIN OF COMMAND

Aide/Para

Steps to take to resolve an issue

Classroom Teacher

Your first step is to meet with your classroom teacher. You want to make them aware of the problem, even if it's a complaint about something they did. Allow the teacher the opportunity to fix the problem before going to the principal or vice principal.

1

Vice Principal or Principal

Your second step is to meet with your site supervisor. Depending on the size of your school, that may entail a vice principal or a principal. If you have a vice principal and principal, exhaust those people before appealing to your union representative or district office support.

2

Union Representative or Human Resources

If your issue is unable to be resolved at the school site, your next best move is to contact your union representative (if you belong to an employee union) or Human Resources. Every school site typically has a representative who can connect you with the appropriate people and advise on the next steps, or if this is not an available option, proceed to Human Resources.

3

ROLE OF THE PARA-PROFESSIONAL AIDE/
CLASSROOM SUPPORT

PARAPROFESSIONALS ARE INVALUABLE SPECIAL EDUCATION TEAM MEMBERS, PROVIDING ESSENTIAL SUPPORT THAT ENHANCES THE EDUCATIONAL EXPERIENCE FOR STUDENTS WITH DISABILITIES.

Their dedication, skills, and collaboration with teachers and other staff ensure that students receive the attention and assistance they need to succeed academically, socially, and emotionally. Understanding your role, in the classroom is critical to a successful learning environment for all.

KEY RESPONSIBILITIES

Instructional Support

Individualized Instruction: Work one-on-one with students to reinforce learning objectives, provide targeted instruction, and adapt lessons to meet individual needs.

Small Group Instruction: Assist small groups of students with assignments and activities, ensuring they understand the material and stay on task.

Classroom Activities: Under the guidance of the special education teacher, help prepare and facilitate classroom activities, projects, and lessons.

Behavioral Support

Behavior Management: Implement behavior management strategies and interventions as outlined in students' Behavior Intervention Plans (BIPs).

Positive Reinforcement: Use positive reinforcement techniques to encourage appropriate behavior and support students in developing social and emotional skills.

Crisis Intervention: Assist in de-escalating situations and providing support during behavioral crises, following established protocols and safety procedures.

CLASSROOM SUPPORT

Personal Care and Assistance

Daily Living Skills: Support students with daily living skills such as eating, dressing, and toileting as needed.

Mobility Assistance: Help students with physical disabilities navigate the classroom and school environment, including transferring to and from wheelchairs or other mobility aids.

Health and Safety: Monitor and address health and safety needs, including administering medications or providing first aid as trained and required.

Academic Support

Assessment Administration: Assist in administering assessments and collecting data on student performance and progress.

Data Collection: Track and record student progress, behaviors, and other relevant information to inform instruction and IEP goals.

Material Preparation: Help prepare instructional materials, modify assignments, and organize resources to support individualized learning plans.

Collaboration

Team Collaboration: Work closely with special education teachers, general education teachers, therapists, and other staff to implement IEPs and support student learning.

Parent Communication: Communicate with parents as directed by the special education teacher, limit this communication I n order to protect yourself from any liabilities.

Professional Development: Participate in training sessions and professional development opportunities to stay informed about best practices and new strategies in special education.

Key Points

You are there as a support to the teacher, **follow their lead but do not be afraid to jump in when a child needs support.**

Limit conversations with parents. Teachers have more training and protections, when it comes to interacting with parents. Besides being a friendly face to greet the child and parent direct all other major questions to the teacher.

Remember that not every day is going to be perfect; your job is to support the teacher and keep students safe. <u>**A positive attitude and flexibility goes a long way!**</u>

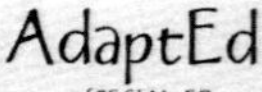

BEST PRACTICES FOR PARAPROFESSIONALS

Build Positive Relationships

Trust and Respect: Develop trusting and respectful relationships with students to create a supportive learning environment.

Empathy and Patience: Show empathy and patience, recognizing the unique challenges and strengths of each student.

Follow Established Plans

IEP Implementation: Adhere to the goals, accommodations, and modifications outlined in each student's Individualized Education Program (IEP).

Consistency: Maintain consistency in implementing behavior plans and instructional strategies as directed by
 the special education teacher.

Stay Informed and Updated

Ongoing Learning: Continuously seek out opportunities for learning and professional growth, including workshops, courses, and conferences.

Feedback: Be open to feedback from teachers and supervisors to improve instructional practices and support strategies.

Maintain Confidentiality

Privacy: Respect the confidentiality of student information and ensure that sensitive details are shared only with authorized personnel. Refrain from discussing a student in front of the student.

Professionalism: Demonstrate professionalism in all interactions with students, parents, and colleagues. Keep your cell phone in your pocket, and do not use it unless you are on a break or in an emergency.

CLASSROOM SUPPORT

IMPACT ON THE CLASSROOM ENVIRONMENT

Enhanced Learning

Paraprofessionals provide crucial support that allows students with disabilities to access the curriculum and participate fully in classroom activities.

Individual Attention

With the help of paraprofessionals, teachers can offer more individualized attention and instruction to students, addressing diverse learning needs.

Positive Behavior Support

Paraprofessionals help create a positive and structured learning environment by implementing behavior management strategies.

Teacher Support

Paraprofessionals enable teachers to focus on planning and delivering instruction by handling many of the day-to-day tasks and individualized support needs.

Inclusive Environment

Paraprofessionals contribute to an inclusive classroom where all students feel supported and valued, promoting social integration and a sense of belonging.